CHAMPIONS OF FREEDOM
Volume 23

AMERICAN PERESTROIKA
THE DEMISE OF THE WELFARE STATE

Richard M. Ebeling, Executive Editor

Lissa Roche and Lorna Busch, General Editors

Hillsdale College Press
Hillsdale, Michigan 49242

Hillsdale College Press
Books by the Hillsdale College Press include The Christian Vision series;
Champions of Freedom series; and other works.

The views expressed in this volume are not necessarily the views of Hillsdale
College.

The Champions of Freedom series
AMERICAN PERESTROIKA
© 1995 by the Hillsdale College Press
Hillsdale, Michigan 49242

Printed in the United States of America

Photo: © 1995 Harvey Finkle and Alan Hinerfeld, Philadelphia, PA

First printing 1995

Library of Congress Catalog Card Number 95-078577

ISBN 0-916308-67-7

CHAMPIONS OF FREEDOM

The Ludwig von Mises Lecture Series

Contents

Contributors

With a law degree from Harvard University, Pete du Pont has served as a state legislator, a U.S. congressman, a two-term governor of Delaware, and in 1988 as a Republican presidential candidate for the presidency of the United States.

During his tenure as Delaware's governor, he signed into law two major income tax reduction measures and a constitutional amendment limiting taxing and spending. He balanced his state budget every year for eight years, and he founded an innovative unemployment prevention program for youths that has since been duplicated in sixteen states and foreign nations. He has also established GOPAC, the only Republican political action committee that works exclusively with candidates for state legislative races. GOPAC has helped more than a thousand individuals run for office and has educated thousands more on how to conduct grassroots political efforts.

Presently, Governor du Pont is a director in a Delaware law firm, policy chairman of the National Center for Policy Analysis, and chairman of the National Review Institute.

Richard M. Ebeling is the Ludwig von Mises Professor of Economics at Hillsdale College. A former professor at the University of Dallas, he joined the Hillsdale faculty in 1988. In addition, he serves on the editorial board of the *Review of Austrian Economics* and as vice president of the Future of Freedom Foundation.

He is the editor of *Money, Method, and the Market Process: Essays by Ludwig von Mises* and a number of volumes in the Hillsdale College Press's Champions of Freedom series, and he is co-editor of *The Dangers of Socialized Medicine.*

Professor Ebeling has lectured extensively on privatization and monetary reform throughout the United States, Latin America, and the former Soviet Union, where he has consulted with the Lithuanian government, the city of Moscow, and the Russian parliament.

David G. Green is director of the Health and Welfare Unit of the Institute of Economic Affairs in London. He carries out in-house research, commissions and edits publications, and serves as a liaison between IEA and the media.

Formerly, he was a research fellow at the Australian National University in Canberra. In 1994, Dr. Green served as a consultant to the New Zealand Business Roundtable, and he has also worked with New Zealand's Task Force on Hospital and Related Services. He is author of articles and essays on politics and social policy which have appeared in such journals as *Economic Affairs, Financial Times* and the *Economist.* His many books include *Reinventing Civil Society: The Rediscovery of Welfare Without Politics* (1993), *Everyone a Private Patient* (1988), and *Working-Class Patients and the Medical Establishment* (1985). He holds a Ph.D. in politics and sociology from the University of Newcastle upon Tyne.

Dwight R. Lee is the Ramsey Professor of Private Enterprise in the department of economics at the University of Georgia. He has also been on the faculty of Washington University-St. Louis, the University of Colorado, Virginia Polytechnic Institute and State University, and George Mason University.

During his career, he has published over eighty articles in academic journals, over one hundred articles and commentaries in magazines and newspapers, and has co-authored seven books and served as the contributing editor of an eighth.

He has also lectured widely throughout the United States as well as Europe, South America and Asia. He received his Ph.D. from the University of California-San Diego.

Charles Murray is the Bradley Fellow at the American Enterprise Institute. He is the author of two of the most important books ever published on welfare and related issues: *Losing Ground: American Social Policy 1950–1980* and *In Pursuit: Of Happiness and Good Government.* He is also co-author of the recently published and highly controversial book, *The Bell Curve: Intelligence and Class Structure in American Life* . He has published regularly in the *New York Times,* the *Wall Street Journal,* the *New Republic,* the *Public Interest, Commentary,* the *Atlantic, National Review* and the *Washington Post.* He has been a featured guest on, among many other programs, *Nightline, This Week with David Brinkley, 20/20,* the *MacNeil/Lehrer NewsHour* and *Firing Line.*

From 1974 through 1981, Murray was a senior scientist at the American Institute for Research, one of the nation's largest private social science research organizations. He supervised evaluations in the fields of urban education, welfare services, adolescent pregnancy, services for the elderly, day-care, and criminal justice. Before joining AIR, Murray spent six years in Thailand, first as a Peace Corps Volunteer, then as a researcher. He holds a B.A. in history from Harvard and a Ph.D. in political science from MIT.

Marvin Olasky is a senior fellow at the Progress and Freedom Foundation and its new Center for Effective Compassion in Washington, D.C. He is also a professor of journalism at the University of Texas at Austin and editor of *World,* a weekly news magazine written from a Christian perspective.

He has written thirteen books, including *The Tragedy of American Compassion, Prodigal Press, Patterns of Corporate Philanthropy* and *Abortion Rites: A Social History of Abortion in America,* as well as more than fifty articles in such journals as *National Review,*

Christianity Today, and *Policy Review.* Dr. Olasky received his B.A. from Yale University and his Ph.D. from the University of Michigan.

Gordon Tullock, who holds a law degree from the University of Chicago, is the Karl Eller Professor of Economics and Political Science at the University of Arizona. He has also taught at Virginia Polytechnic Institute and State University, the University of Virginia, the University of South Carolina, Rice University, and George Mason University, and under the United States Foreign Service, has served as a consulate and embassy officer in China and Korea.

Currently, he is on the board of editors of the *Journal of Social and Biological Structure,* the *International Journal of Law and Economics,* and the *Atlantic Economic Journal.* In 1993, he was presented the Adam Smith Award in Washington, D.C. and is the first recipient of the Leslie T. Wilkins Award presented for "The Outstanding Book in the Field of Criminology and Criminal Justice" by the Criminal Justice Research Center.

He has edited, written, and co-edited twenty-four books, which include *The Calculus of Consent: Logical Foundations of a Constitutional Democracy* (1962), *The Politics of Bureaucracy* (1987), *Wealth, Poverty, and Politics* (1988), and *The New World of Economics: Explorations into the Human Experience* (1992), which is now in its sixth edition and has been translated into Spanish, German, and Japanese.

Richard E. Wagner is the Holbert R. Harris Professor of Economics and past chairman of the department of economics at George Mason University, where he has taught since 1988. He is also a member of the editorial boards of two leading academic journals, *Public Choice* and the *Supreme Court Economic Review.*

Dr. Wagner has taught at the University of California-Irvine, Tulane University, Virginia Polytechnic Institute and State University, Auburn University, and Florida State University.

His writings, which have covered a broad range of topics on matters of political economy and public policy, have resulted in a total of twenty books and over one hundred articles in scholarly journals. His books include *Public Debt in a Democratic Society* and *Democracy in Deficit* (both co-authored with Nobel laureate James Buchanan), *To Promote the General Welfare, Inheritance and the State* and *Parchment, Guns and Constitutional Order.* He earned his B.S. from the University of Southern California and his Ph.D. from the University of Virginia.

Gary Wolfram is the George Munson Professor of Political Economy at Hillsdale College and president of the Hillsdale Policy Group, a private consulting firm that specializes in public policy analysis. He is also a member of the Michigan State Board of Education and the Michigan Enterprise Zone Authority. Currently, Dr. Wolfram is on leave from the College, serving as administrative assistant to Representative Nick Smith (R-MI).

In the past, he served as Michigan's deputy state treasurer for taxation and economic policy, as chairman of the Headlee Amendment Blue Ribbon Commission, as senior economist to the Republican members of the state senate, and as senior economist to Representative Nick Smith. Dr. Wolfram holds a bachelor's degree from the University of California-Santa Barbara and a doctorate from the University of California-Berkeley. He has taught at Mount Holyoke College, the University of Michigan, and Washington State University. His publications include several works on Michigan's tax structure.

Gleaves Whitney is speech writer to Michigan Governor John Engler, and he also serves as the Governor's liaison to conservative foundations and institutions. In 1993 he served on the Governor's task force on education, whose work led to the enactment of far-reaching reforms that the *New York Times* called "the most dramatic in the nation."

He attended the University of Colorado and, after completing his undergraduate studies, had his first history text published, called *Colorado Front Range* (1983). He went on to Germany as a member of the Fulbright program to teach English and American Studies and then to Oxford to continue his education. At the University of Michigan, he is currently completing his doctoral dissertation in history.

In addition to his work with Governor Engler, Mr. Whitney serves on the National Policy Forum and is the Michigan spokesman for the Catholic Campaign for America. His work has appeared in the *Wall Street Journal, National Review,* the *Christian Science Monitor, Vital Speeches,* the *Intercollegiate Review,* and the *University Bookman.* In addition, he has written six articles in the *Encyclopedia of the American Right* (forthcoming).

Introduction

Sixty years after Roosevelt's New Deal and thirty years after Johnson's Great Society, the American welfare state has grown to vast proportions and has created a $50-billion-a-year "poverty industry." It is a complete failure. It strangles the economy and encourages a vicious cycle of amorality and dependency. Its unemployment benefits subsidize joblessness. Its taxes prevent capital formation and the creation of new businesses, jobs, goods, and services. And its regulations impose billions of dollars of added costs on the private sector and hence on every member of society.

The welfare state has not proven to be a solution to our problems; it has only made them worse. But throughout the last several decades, its advocates continued to insist that we could "reform" welfare—by expanding it. Their political triumph meant throwing more dollars at a failing system, staving off genuine reform, and dooming the hopes of those trapped in the "permanent underclass."

Now, in the 1990s, genuine reforms are finally being attempted. Michigan has abolished General Assistance programs. New Jersey provides no new aid for mothers who have children while on welfare, and it offers generous benefits for those who marry or go to work. Ohio docks payments to teen mothers who don't regularly attend school. Wyoming forces fathers of AFDC children to pay child support. And Wisconsin has passed a law that will end welfare by 1998 and set up an alternative system. It has already cut welfare rolls and put more people back to work than any other state. And in the fall of 1993, a seminal *Wall Street Journal* article by Charles Murray boldly proposed the abolition of all welfare across America.

This volume in Hillsdale College's Champions of Freedom series explores the past, present, and future of welfare. It is based on lectures presented during the Center for Constructive Alternatives and Ludwig von Mises Lecture Series seminar, "American Perestroika: The Demise of the Welfare State," held in March 1995.

—The Editors

October 1995
Hillsdale College

Richard M. Ebeling

The Political Myths and Economic Realities of the Welfare State

The Origin of the Modern Welfare State

Austrian economist Ludwig von Mises began his 1922 treatise on *Socialism* with the observation that, "Socialism is the watchword and the catchword of the day. The socialist idea dominates the modern spirit. The masses approve of it, it expresses the thoughts and the feelings of all; it has set its seal upon our time. When history comes to tell our story it will write above the chapter, 'The Epoch of Socialism.'"[1]

It may seem that the socialist epoch has now come to a close. Nothing is in greater disrepute at the present time than the idea of government ownership of the means of production and the theory of comprehensive central planning. The material and spiritual destructiveness of the socialist ideal is too visible in Eastern Europe and the former Soviet Union for anyone seriously to propose a return to the total state as it has been experienced in this century, either in its fascist or communist variation. Maybe the next century will see the renewal of its appeal under some new ideological garb. The appeal of utopia, unfortunately, seems indestructible.[2] But for now, utopian collectivism is in hiatus.

However, the ghost of socialism past still haunts the present. That ghost of socialism past is the modern welfare state. Even

3

in the face of the failure of Soviet-style socialism, the ideas that were the foundations upon which the Marxian scourge came to plague the globe still dominate and guide the thinking of social and economic policy in practically every country in the world. The reason for this is simple. The modern welfare state emerged as an attempt to meet the challenge of socialism's critique of the market economy, without the necessity for socialism's radical medicine for revolutionary transformation of society.

The birthplace of modern welfare statism was Imperial Germany during the last decades of the nineteenth century, in the reign of Wilhelm II and the administration of Chancellor Otto von Bismarck.[3] In the 1870s, the German Social Democratic Party had acquired increasing support among the German electorate and threatened to obtain a majority in the Reichstag, the German Parliament.[4] The electoral triumph of Germany's socialist party seemed likely in the near future. The German monarchy and the conservative parties realized that something had to be done to deflect popular support away from the socialists and back to the established order.

In the early 1880s, Kaiser Wilhelm agreed to sponsor the first welfare statist legislation that was enacted by the Reichstag. In the 1890s, Bismarck explained his tactical goal to William H. Dawson, an American historian and Bismarckian sympathizer: "My idea was to bribe the working classes, or shall I say, to win them over, to regard the state as a social institution existing for their sake and interested in their welfare. It is not moral to make profits out of human misfortunes and suffering," he concluded. "Life-insurance, accident insurance, sickness insurance should not be subjects of private speculation. They should be carried out by the state or at least insurance should be on the mutual principle and no dividends or profits should be derived by private persons."[5]

But it would be a mistake to interpret the birth of the modern welfare state as purely a cynical political pragmatism. It was also argued on the basis of a supposed higher "social good" and a higher conception of human liberty than a "mere" protection of life, liberty and property by the state. The proponents of this view were known as the German Historical School, leading members of which were Gustav von Schmoller, Adolph Wagner, Lujo Brentano and a host of others who are now long forgotten, but who were extremely influential at the time in developing the political, economic, and ethical rationales for the welfare state.[6] They rejected radical or Marxian socialism and advocated, instead, what they called state socialism.[7] William H. Dawson explained the difference:

> While Individualism restricts the functions of the state as much as possible, Socialism enlarges them; the Individualist would do everything without the state, the socialist would do everything with it. State socialism is the mean between these directions of thought; in it the two extremes meet....Socialism would abolish the existing political order altogether, while State Socialism would use the state for the accomplishment of great economic and social purposes, especially restoring to it the function, which Frederick the Great held to be the principle business of the state, of "holding the balance" between classes and parties....The nonintervention principle must be abandoned, since it has only led to greater and ever greater class and personal inequalities, and therefore to growing social disorganization and discontent....Social interests can only be properly safeguarded when the state directly concerns itself with them. The aim must, therefore, be to widen the economic jurisdiction of the state.[8]

State socialism was meant to save the established order from revolutionary upheaval and societal disintegration by admitting many of the criticisms that socialists made against a market economy—exploitation of the workers by the employers, self-interested behavior that failed to serve the general welfare, poverty of the many in the midst of material riches enjoyed by a few—and introducing a series of interventionist and welfarist policies that were to improve the economic lot of "the masses."9

The comprehensiveness of the German welfare state was emphasized in 1915 by another American admirer, Frederic C. Howe (a prominent intellectual who played a leading role in the Progressive movement and later served in Franklin Roosevelt's New Deal):

> The [German] state has its finger on the pulse of the worker from the cradle to the grave. His education, his health, and his working efficiency are matters of constant concern. He is carefully protected from accident by laws and regulations governing factories. He is trained in his hand and his brain to be a good workman and is insured against accident, sickness, and old age. While idle through no fault of his own, work is frequently found for him. When homeless, a lodging is offered so that he will not easily pass to the vagrant class. When sick, he is cared for in wonderful convalescent homes, tuberculosis hospitals, and farm colonies. When old age removes him from the mill or factory, a pension awaits him, a slight mark of appreciation from society, which has taken in labor all that his life had to give and left him with nothing more than a bare subsistence wage.10

Frederic Howe admitted that under this system, with its pervasive controls and regulations, "The individual exists for the state, not the state for the individual." But he went on to explain that in this German welfare paradise, the people did not lose freedom, rather they had a different kind of freedom than in America. "This paternalism does not necessarily mean less freedom to the individual than that which prevails in America or England. It is rather a different kind of freedom," Howe said. "[T]he German enjoys a freedom far greater than that which prevails in America or England. This freedom is of an economic sort....Social legislation directed against the exploitation of the worker and the consumer insures freedom in many other ways. It protects the defenseless classes from exploitation and abuse. It safeguards the weak. Universal education offers opportunities to even the poorest to advance whether it be in the service of the state or in the fields of individual effort. Germany protects industrial and social equality...."[11]

Furthermore, Howe explained that the principle guiding the policies of the welfare state was *expediency*. "In the mind of the Germans, the functions of the state are not susceptible to abstract, a priori deductions. Each proposal must be decided by the time and the conditions," he said. "If it seems advisable for the state to own an industry it should proceed to own it; if it is wise to curb any class or interest it should be curbed. Expediency or opportunism is the rule of statesmanship, not abstraction as to the philosophical nature of the state."[12]

To promulgate and diffuse these ideas, members of the German Historical School founded in 1872 a professional association called the *Verein für Sozialpolitik* (Society for Social Policy). The opening address was given by Gustav von Schmoller, who emphasized that their purpose as a group was to see that "'a constantly increasing portion of our people shall share in the great possessions of civilization, in culture and material welfare'....But such an end cannot be attained by the uncontrolled struggle of class against class and individual against individual, nor by the power of an all-embracing and all-controlling state. The state must be the regulator and moderator of the contending industrial classes, 'the greatest moral institution for the education of human kind.' Therefore, the state must have strength and power. Standing above the selfish interests of classes, it must enact laws, direct the community with a just hand, and protect the weak, raise the humble."[13]

The idea and the ideology of the modern welfare state began to reach across the Atlantic to the shores of America in those last decades of the nineteenth century. Beginning from the 1870s through the turn of the century a significant number of American social scientists—political scientists, sociologists and economists—enrolled in German universities to acquire their Ph.D.s and to complete post-doctoral studies. Germany was viewed not only as the land of poets and philosophers, but as the most advanced and progressive nation in the world in terms of social thinking and enlightened public policy. The German university became the Mecca of all dedicated and "forward-looking" young scholars.[14]

By the beginning of the twentieth century, almost a hundred American economists who were considered prominent in the economics profession at the time had studied at German universities during their younger years.[15] In 1885, some of these German-trained economists decided to follow the lead of their teachers, and they founded their own professional economic society: The American Economic Association. Wesley C. Mitchell has explained that:

> The organizers were personally eager that the association should take the general attitude toward economics which was dominant in the Germany of their time, an attitude that was commonly characterized as "Socialism of the Chair." At that time the historical school was growing rapidly in Germany. It laid great stress upon the state as an institution, upon the role that it was destined to play in human life....These people took a bold attitude regarding the duties of the economists to participate in the great tasks of the state of shaping culture into forms that were worthy of man's high destiny. Ideas of this sort cropped up in the third article in the Constitution [of the American Economic Association] called "Statement of Principles." It begins as follows: "We regard the state as an agency whose positive assistance is one of the indispensable conditions of human progress."...The statement went on: "We believe that political economy as a science is still in an early stage of development....While we appreciate the work of former economists, we look not so much to speculation as to the historical and statistical study of actual conditions of eco-

nomic life for the satisfactory accomplishment of that development."...The next point was: "We hold that the conflict of labor and capital has brought into prominence a vast number of social problems, whose solution requires the united efforts, each in its own sphere, of the church, of the state and of science."...The last point read: "In the study of the industrial and commercial policy of governments we take no partisan attitude. We believe in a progressive development of economic conditions, which must be met by a corresponding development of legislative policy."[16]

The ideas of these economists, and those of their colleagues in the neighboring fields of political science and sociology soon served as the foundation for the welfare statist ideas that came to predominate in American public policy discussions in the period known as the Progressive Era.[17] Indeed, the entire assumptions from which economists thought about human welfare and public policy experienced a sea-change in a matter of a couple of decades. For example, in 1887, J. Laurence Laughlin, who founded the economics department at the University of Chicago, could still say in his textbook, *The Elements of Political Economy*:

> Socialism, or the reliance on the state for help, stands in antagonism to *self-help*, or the activity of the individual. That body of people certainly is the strongest and the happiest in which each person is thinking for himself, is independent, self-respecting, self-confident, self-controlled, self-mastered. Whenever a man does a thing for himself he values it infinitely more than if it is done for him, and he a better man for having done it....The man who hews out his own path gains power by so doing, and becomes self-reliant, sagacious, foresighted, and ready for further advance....If, on the other hand, men constantly hear it said that they are oppressed and downtrodden, deprived of their own, ground down by the rich, and that the state

will set all things right for them in time, what other effect can that teaching have on the character and energy of the ignorant than the complete destruction of all self-help? They begin to think that they can have commodities which they have not helped to produce. They begin to believe that two and two make five. It is for this reason that *socialistic teaching strikes at the root of individuality and independent character,* and lowers the self-respect of men who ought to be taught self-reliance....The danger of enervating results flowing from dependence on the state for help should cause us to *restrict the interference of legislation as far as is possible;* it should be permitted only when there is an absolute necessity, and even then it should be undertaken with hesitation....The right policy is a matter of supreme importance, and we should not like to see in our country the system of interference as exhibited in the paternal theory of government existing in France and Germany.[18]

But in the years just before the First World War, this was no longer the dominant view among economists. Any number of prominent economists from this period could be quoted to give a flavor of the "new thinking." I choose Henry Seager of Columbia University, who had gone to Europe in 1892 and spent a term at the University of Berlin studying with Gustav von Schmoller, and then spent a term at the University of Vienna studying with the Austrian economists, Carl Menger and Eugen von Böhm-Bawerk, but who came back to America primarily influenced on matters of public policy by the German Historical School.[19]

The closing chapters of his popular and widely used 1913 textbook, *Principles of Economics,* were devoted to a detailed analysis and justification for government intervention in the areas of labor unions, limitations on women's and children's labor, minimum wage laws, and compulsory accident, sickness, and unemployment insurance, in which the "progressive" state programs in Imperial Germany were presented as models for

America to emulate.[20] Consistent with his German mentors, Seager explained the unrealistic utopianism and societal danger embedded in the arguments for radical socialism. What was needed was a moderate social-welfare reformism that would ameliorate the class and social conflicts that the socialists were right to cite:

> Although as regards the ultimate goal of economic progress there is a wide difference between socialists and nonsocialists, as regards the next steps in social advance all progressive thinkers on economic problems can make common cause. That progress must be away from the present gross inequalities in opportunity and wealth toward greater equality is the view of not only socialists, but of all economists and social reformers. That a chief means of effecting such progress must be a widening of the functions of the state in the direction of further limitations on the rights of property and the more rigid regulation of industries is also a conviction commonly shared. In fact, there is so little difference as regards their attitude toward the practical problems of the day between evolutionary socialists and progressive social reformers that it is often difficult to tell one from the other....Nonsocialists can see no reason to assign such an all-embracing role to the state in the industrial society of the future, but agree that there is urgent need of social reform in the present and that all should work together to secure it.[21]

By the time of the First World War, socialism was triumphant over the minds of intellectuals and an increasing number of policymakers throughout Europe and North America. Even for those who had rejected the notion of radical, revolutionary upheaval to overturn the prevailing social order, the socialist idea had captured their soul.[22] Why? Because they had accepted the premises upon which the socialist ideal was constructed. The market economy was accepted as the source of unjustifiable inequality of income and status in society. The institution of private property was viewed as the source of social conflict and the exploitation of those luckless enough to be without legal title to any of the means of production. The market economy failed to reward the "working class" with a sufficient remuneration to secure their own requirements for the vicissitudes of injury, old-age, and periodic episodes of unemployment.

And most importantly, the state was viewed as the institution of society that could and would harmonize the interests of a multitude of conflicting social and economic interests for a higher common societal welfare. The classical economists of the early nineteenth century had been critical of state intervention into market relationships. They doubted that the political authority had either the knowledge or the wisdom to manage the complex and changing currents of market activity effectively. And they were suspicious of governments having the power to bestow privileges on some and penalties on others, because, though the arguments for such bounties and prohibitions were couched in the language of serving the "public interest," they understood that the actual purpose behind it was usually to serve some special interest at the expense of the society as a whole.[23]

Now the state was to be the great savior of society, the cure for all its ills. All we needed to do was work together for the greater good. Is this an exaggeration? Here are the words of Richard Ely, professor of economics at the University of Wisconsin, cofounder of the American Economic Association and a leader of the welfare statist reform movement in the United States. He concluded his 1895 book on socialism and reform with the following hope and vision:

> Looking into the future we may contemplate a society with real, not merely nominal, freedom, to pursue the best; a society in which men shall work together for the

common purposes, and in which the wholesale cooperation shall take place largely through government, but
through a government which has become less repressive
and has developed its positive side. We have reason to
believe that we shall yet see great national undertakings
with the property of the nation, and managed by the
nation, through agents who appreciate the glory of true
public service, and feel that it is God's work which they
are doing, because church and state are as one. We may
look forward to a society in which education, art, and literature shall be fostered by the nation, and in which the
federal government, commonwealth, local community,
and individual citizens shall heartily cooperate for the
advancement of civilization....We may anticipate an
approximation of state and society as men improve, and
we may hope that men outside of government will freely
and voluntarily act with trained officers and experts in
the service of government for the advancement of common interests.[24]

In the society of the future, men would rise to a higher level
of consciousness and employ themselves in government, seeing themselves doing God's work and not for anything as narrow as their own self-interest. The distinction between civil
society and the political authority would be obliterated, with
private affairs and matters of state being indistinguishable and
indeed practically interchangeable. Not only would the material concerns of old age, sickness, and unemployment be
secured from the cradle to the grave but so, too, would be the
concerns of the spirit and the mind—education, art, literature.
Here was the alternative offered by the welfare statists in place
of the radical upheaval preached by their more extreme socialist cousins: moderate utopia by political increment and democratic consensus.

The Political-Economic Reality of the Welfare State

The West, including the United States, has been in the grip of the welfare state for more than three-quarters of a century. Wages and prices in many industries are either controlled, regulated, or influenced by government. Methods of production and rules for the marketing and sale of goods and services are prescribed by governmental laws and decrees. The income earned by many is seized through taxation by the state and distributed to numerous privileged groups and special interests. A vast bureaucracy oversees and manages the affairs of millions in practically every aspect of personal, social and economic life. The state is everywhere. And the state intrudes into everything. There is hardly a corner of life in which the state does not penetrate and take a hand.[25]

The ideal of welfare statists like Richard Ely and Henry Seager has become reality. The distinction between society and the state has not become nonexistent, but has become significantly diminished. Are you poor and unskilled? Don't try to work for less than the minimum wage; the government will come down on the employer with all its might. Want to work for an employer who would be glad to hire you? If it is a unionized industry, state and federal authorities will do everything in their power to stop you, unless you join the union and pay dues for union services that you may neither want nor agree with. Want to work at home on contract for some employer? The federal government has banned many forms of "cottage industries" as "exploitation," no matter how convenient and profitable it may be for both you and your employer.

Forget about being self-employed in many cities if you have in mind driving you own taxi cab. This is a monopoly privilege for those lucky or wealthy enough to obtain the necessary government license. If you want to pursue one of dozens of various careers, you will find the same licensing restrictions; for the privileged few in these and similar professions, licensing assures smaller supplies and higher prices than a more open market would provide.

You think you own your property and that it is constitutionally protected from unreasonable search or seizure? In the name of fighting organized crime and the drug cartels, the state has imposed forfeiture laws that enable government at practically every level to seize any of your property under any vague suspicion in the mind of a government agent that your property was acquired illegally; and the burden of proof falls on you—the accused victim—to prove that you are not guilty; and even if you succeed, don't expect an easy time getting your property back.

You consider that your home is your castle? Just try to remodel or modify it or add any structures to it without appropriate zoning ordinance approval; and, even if the approval is acquired, it may be revoked after the construction work has been done. You can also be stopped from doing anything with your property if it is declared to be a historical landmark.[26]

Affirmative-action laws and the Americans with Disabilities Act have become swamps of political privilege and plunder with which, in the name of equal opportunity and equal treatment, the state has the power to treat people unequally. And the power to make decisions is held by bureaucrats possessing their own prejudices, biases, political pressures, and imperfections of knowledge.[27]

Find yourself on welfare assistance? If you are a man, the state may drive you from the household. If you are a woman, it may encourage you to have children born out of wedlock. And it may create disincentives for getting off the welfare assistance, and manipulate where and how you live.[28]

The examples that I have enumerated go beyond the narrow conception that many people have of the welfare state, under which government welfare is usually thought of meaning those unemployed and in a low income category who receive various forms of cash and in-kind assistance from the state. The welfare statists in the late nineteenth and early twentieth century had no such narrow or limited conception.[29] As we saw, they desired every facet of life to be "reformed" and integrated into a structure of "social policy." The rights to property were to be weakened to make the use of property conform to some conception of the "public interest." They viewed the free, unregulated market as an arena of exploitation, abuse and injustice; as a consequence every aspect of market activity would have to be open to intervention and regulation by the state for the benefit of the "good of society" as a whole. And there were no rough and ready rules for the types or degrees of intervention, these were matters of ever-changing expediency, which they viewed as the mark of true "statesmanship." Pragmatism and "opportunism" were the principles that were to lived by in the New Era of the welfare state. We have been living in that New Era and those have been the principles that have guided the political process. The characteristics of the modern welfare state can be looked at under three headings: "Bourgeois Socialism," the "Welfare State Nomenklatura" and the "Hubris of the Intellectuals."

Bourgeois Socialism

Since the welfare state in all its modern complexity only developed in pragmatic increments over several generations, we now have a generation of people in both Western Europe and North America who cannot even conceive of a world without the welfare state. It seems "natural," the normal state of affairs to which any reasonable person should take no exception. Indeed, most people, while they may complain or even disapprove of some particular program financed by the state, think that the institutional order of the welfare state *is* the free society and *is* a free market economy. What people cannot see clearly is what the Italian economist and sociologist Vilfredo Pareto tried to explain a hundred years ago, in 1891, as his native Italy was already beginning on the road to the modern welfare state: "The actual condition of civil society, as it is today, is based not on free competition and respect for private property, but on the intervention of the state. So the governments of civilized peoples can be defined as bourgeois socialist." If the use of the word socialist in this manner shocked his readers at the time, he suggested, "A looser definition could be that socialism wants the intervention of the state to change the distribution of wealth," with socialists "divided into two types: socialists, who through intervention of the state, wish to change the distribution of income in favor of the less rich; and the others, who, even if they are sometimes not completely conscious of what they are doing, favor the rich."[30]

The particular and peculiar characteristics of the modern Bourgeois Socialist welfare state can be best understood if it is contrasted with the system of redistributive welfare statism that existed before the nineteenth century, a system that was known as mercantilism.[31] In the eighteenth century, political privileges and favors were primarily bestowed upon a few select members of the society: landowners who were given agricultural protection from the competition of less expensive food suppliers in other countries; and particular merchants and manufacturers who were given the monopoly privileges to buy, sell and trade various goods and services. The vast majority of the society paid for the protections and privileges given to the few. They paid in the form of higher prices, inferior products and fewer consumer choices in the market. And their meager income and wealth were severely taxed not only to pay for the state subsidies of selected industries and exports, but also to finance the governmental bureaucracy that supervised it all.

The success of the nineteenth-century free trade movement, especially in England, was partly due to the fact that the advocates of economic liberty could point to the injustice of a system that gave privileges to a few, while making the majority of the people bear the burden. Mercantilism went against the grain of the new beliefs in political democracy and equal treatment before the law.

With the spread of the democratic ideal and the enlargement of the voting franchise, people increasingly came to view government as no longer the master, but rather as the servant. But a servant for what? For equal protection before the law, certainly. For equality in civil liberties, increasingly. But unfortunately, *with the spread of socialist ideas in the late nineteenth and early twentieth centuries, government also came to be viewed as an agency that should do things for the people, rather than only protecting them from the violence or fraud of others.*

And what people were told they should want government to do for them was: guarantee their jobs and income; protect them from foreign competition and limit the entry of new competitors at home; assure them "living wages" for their labor and "fair" and "reasonable" prices for their products; protect them from the common mistakes and misfortunes of everyday life; and relieve them of any responsibility for the community efforts that would otherwise demand of them charity and the giving of their own free time. *And all of these guarantees, protections and securities were to be provided at someone else's expense.*

As the ideal of a welfare-providing government for the people spread, those who hoped to gain some privileges from the government formed themselves into groups of common economic interest. In this way, they aimed to pool the costs of the lobbying and politicking that was required to obtain what they increasingly came to view as their "right," i.e., those things to which they were told they were "entitled."

No longer were redistributive privileges to be limited to the few, as under the old mercantilism. No, now privileges and favors were to be available for all. Bourgeois Socialism, therefore, heralded a new age, an Age of Democratized Privilege and it now permeates the Western world. More and more people are dependent upon governmental spending of one form or another for significant portions of their income. And what the government does not redistribute directly, it furnishes indirectly through industrial regulations, price and production controls, and occupational licensing procedures.

As dependency upon the state has expanded, the incentives to resist any diminution in either governmental spending or intervention has increased. All cuts in government spending and repeals of interventions threaten an immediate and significant reduction in the incomes of the affected, privileged groups. And since all of the benefits to society which accrue from greater market competition and self-responsibility are not immediate but rather are spread over a period of time, there are few present-day advocates of a comprehensive reversal of all that makes up the modern welfare state.

Instead, practically every group in society continuously does battle for the maintenance of, or an increase in, their piece of the economic pie—not through open competition for consumer business, but through the political process to gain a larger share through direct wealth redistribution or manipulation of the market.

This is not the process or the result that the proponents of the welfare state saw or promised, when they first were making the case for their form of moderate utopianism a hundred years ago. Why have democratic societies all around the world become battlegrounds for political privilege and economic plunder?

The answer is to be found in one of the ideas that Adam Smith did so much to popularize: the division of labor. "The division of labor," Smith explained, "so far as it can be introduced, occasions in every art, a proportionate increase of the productive powers of labor."[32] By specializing in various lines of production, the members of society are able to improve and increase their skills and efficiency to do various things. Out of these productive specializations comes an increased supply of all kinds of goods and services. The members of society trade away the larger quantities of each commodity they respectively can now produce for all the other goods offered by their fellows in the market arena. Society's members give up the independence of economic self-sufficiency for the interdependence of a social system of division of labor. But the gain is a much higher standard of living than any one of them could ever hope to attain just by using his own capabilities to fulfill all his wants and desires through his own labor.[33]

Each individual is now dependent upon others in the society

for the vast majority of the goods and services he wishes to use and consume. But in a competitive market setting, this works to his advantage. Sellers vie with one another for his consumer business. They underbid each other and offer him attractively lower prices; they devise ways to produce and market new and improved products. As a consumer, the individual is the master of the market, whom all sellers must serve if they are to obtain his business. Viewed from the perspective of the consumer, the competitive market serves the public interest. The resources of society are effectively applied and put to work to satisfy the various wants and desires of the individuals of that society. The products which are manufactured are determined by the free choices of all the demanders in the marketplace. Production serves consumption.

But the market looks totally different from the perspective of the individual producers. They, too, are dependent upon the market; they are dependent upon buyers being willing to purchase what they have for sale. While the market serves every one as a consumer, no one can be a consumer unless he has been successful as a producer. And his success as a producer depends upon his ability to market and sell his products, or to find willing employers for his particular labor skills and abilities. As a consequence, for each producer the price of his own product or labor service tends to be more important to him than the prices of all the multitude of consumer goods he might purchase. Unless he earns the necessary financial wherewithal in his producer role, he cannot be a consumer of what others have for sale.

Being a consumer of many things, but the producer of usually one thing, each seller tends to view competition as a financial threat to his position in the market, as well as his specific share of the market. The incentive for each producer, therefore, is to want to limit entry into his corner of the market, or to reduce the amount of competition currently existing in his industry or profession. The only avenue for limiting competition, however, is the government. Only the government has the ultimate authority to prohibit permanently those who think they could do better in the market and who desire to try. Producers, therefore, have incentives to apply portions of the resources and wealth at their disposal for use in the political arena to gain or protect the market position they feel themselves unable to obtain or protect in a open field of competition. And as long as the costs of acquiring political privileges, protections, and redistributions from the government are less than those of acquiring desired wealth through the voluntary transactions and associations on the market, producers have incentives to lobby and politick to achieve their ends.[34]

The Welfare State Nomenklatura

In the political process of the welfare state, Bourgeois Socialism has both an accomplice and a rival. This accomplice and rival can be called the Welfare State Nomenklatura. "Nomenklatura" is a Soviet term. It referred to those who wielded power and authority in the bureaucracy that oversaw and controlled the Soviet economy.[35] If the state is to regulate and control the market, supervise the condition and improvement of the poor, redistribute wealth, oversee the education of our children, plan the arrangement of cities and the preservation of the environment, subsidize the arts and prohibit or restrict access to "socially harmful" substances, then there must be a group of "trained officers and experts in the service of government for the advancement of common interests," whom Richard Ely expected to be agents motivated by "the glory of true public service."

It was typical of the socialist illusion that underlies the welfare statist rationale that it was presumed that the motives for human behavior were determined by the cultural and social environment. In the beautiful future of social reform, men would no longer think only or even predominantly of their own interests. No, the "experts" employed in the state agencies and bureaus, who were to be responsible for the remaking of society, would have but one purpose: the common interest. And "men outside of government will freely and voluntarily act" with these selfless agents of the public interest for a greater common good than their own private gain and improvement.[36]

Yet the performance of the functions of the state are actually one of the specializations in the social system of division of labor. It is a source of income and power for those who occupy these positions of political authority and responsibility. Advancement, increased income, and expanded jurisdiction as means for personal improvement all require the ever-renewed justification for their bureau or agency. Their relative income and relative power in the political arena depend upon the proof that their activity needs to be continued or expanded.

The private entrepreneur in the free market searches out unsatisfied consumer wants that he tries to fulfill better than any rival. The "product" the members of the Welfare State Nomenklatura must sell is their competency to rectify or prevent the supposed "failures" of the market. Indeed, they must constantly be on the lookout for new market failures. They specialize in the discovery of "social crises" that a free market and voluntary associations supposedly cannot cure. Just as private entrepreneurs may creatively come up with new products that they believe consumers have never had available to them before, the members of the Welfare State Nomenklatura creatively come up with new social problems needing a political cure; and, of course, they are regarded as the public-interested experts most competent to take on the new task. Their bread and butter depend upon the never-ending demonstration that freedom and the free market neither satisfactorily work nor can be fully trusted.

And as they pursue the expansion of their power over the redistribution of wealth and the regulation of private enterprise, they have need of allies and outside "experts" to assist them in their own lobbying for increased jurisdiction and enhanced budgets. Those in the private sector who desire to use the state for their own Bourgeois Socialist goals of obtaining subsidies, restrictions on domestic and foreign competition, and favorable pricing or production regulations, offer their expertise to demonstrate that only through such policies can the national interest be served; their particular sectorial interests, by happy coincidence, are just what serves the public interest.

Yet, the interests of the Welfare State Nomenklatura are not merely a reflection of private special interests of the Bourgeois Socialists. Their source of power is the authority to control or influence relative prices, regulate the permitted methods of production and sale of goods and services in the market, and to determine the allocation of redistributed wealth. This requires control over private enterprise and not obedient subservience to the special interest groups over whom they have or want jurisdiction.

At the same time, the desire and the need to interact with the Welfare State Nomenklatura further corrupts the behavior and incentives of those private enterprisers that function in this politicized market environment. Political connections and knowing how to maneuver in the welfare statist environment can come to have equal or even greater significance for financial success than that of normal market acumen. What such a hyper-politicized market can come to look like was explained by Ludwig von Mises in 1932, in a description of business activity in Germany at the end of the Weimar Republic shortly before the arrival of the Nazis to power:

> In the interventionist state it is no longer of crucial importance for the success of an enterprise that operations be run in such a way that the needs of the consumer are satisfied in the best and least expensive way; it is much more important that one has "good relations" with the controlling political factions, that the interventions redound to the advantage and not the disadvantage of the enterprise. A few more Marks' worth of tariff-protection for the out-

put of the enterprise, a few Marks less tariff protection for the inputs in the manufacturing process can help the enterprise more than the greatest prudence in the conduct of the operations. An enterprise may be well run, but it will go under if it does not know how to protect its interests in the arrangement of the tariff rates, in the wage negotiations before arbitration boards, and in governing bodies of cartels. It is much more important to have "connections" than to produce well and cheaply. Consequently, the men who reach the top of such enterprises are not those who know how to organize operations and give production a direction which the market situation demands, but rather men who are in good standing both "above" and "below," men who know how to get along with the press and with all the political parties, especially with the radicals, such that their deals cause no offense. This is that class of general directors who deal more with federal dignitaries and party leaders than with those from whom they buy and to whom they sell.

Because many ventures depend on political favors, those who undertake such ventures must repay the politicians with favors. There has been no big venture in recent years which has not had to expend considerable sums for transactions which from the outset were clearly unprofitable but which, despite expected losses, had to be concluded for political reasons. This is not to mention contributions to nonbusiness concerns—election funds, public welfare institutions and the like.[37]

Hubris of the Intellectuals

Political plunder, state-bestowed monopolies and forced redistribution of wealth are nothing new in human history. Yet what has been unique for more than a hundred years has been the arrogance of those who have proposed to modify the outcomes of the free society into directions that they think superior to the ones that naturally emerge out of the voluntary associations and mutually agreed upon transactions of the participants of the market. Let us turn, once more, to Richard Ely. He asked the question:

> Can we not, in our industrial life, keep what we have that is valuable and escape some of the evils which socialism has so vividly depicted? And let us frankly, fully, without equivocation, acknowledge the great services which socialism has, in this as in other respects, rendered to society. Can we not carefully, conservatively add to our social order some of the strong features of socialism, and yet to keep this social order intact? It seems to the author that this is practicable, and the means for doing this he endeavors to describe as a program of practicable reform....Those who take up social reform at the present day, must remember that they cannot accomplish much that is permanently valuable unless they start with a full knowledge of socialism and its advantages, and attempt to realize these advantages....Well-directed effort has accomplished great things; and we are warranted in the belief that a thorough reformation of society, and the reduction of social evils to a very low term, if not a complete abolition, is practicable.[38]

What were the important lessons that socialism supposedly had to teach us? Karl Marx and Frederick Engels, Ely believed, had shown that if not restrained by government controls, under a free market "the conditions of the wage earners would have grown more and more wretched, the concentration of wealth and the centralization of production would have been carried even further, and it is not improbable that the collapse" of capitalism would have taken place. Only enlightened state intervention and redistribution of wealth could and had prevented this from happening.

What did enlightened reformers need to do through the agency of government? "First of all, we must seek a better utilization of productive forces," Ely said. "This implies, negatively, that we should reduce the waste of the competitive system to its lowest possible terms; positively, that we should endeavor to secure a steady production, employing all available capital and labor power....In the second place, would we secure the advantages of socialism," Ely continued, "we must so mend our distribution of wealth that we shall avoid present extremes, and bring about widely diffused comfort, making frugal comfort for all an aim. Distribution must be so shaped, if practicable, that all shall have assured incomes....In the third place, there must be abundant public provision of opportunities for the development of our faculties, including educational facilities and the large use of natural resources for purposes of recreation."[39]

These have been the premises and goals of the welfare state during the twentieth century. Karl Marx arrogantly labeled his ideas, "scientific socialism" because he claimed to have discovered the laws of history that made the passing of capitalism and the arrival of socialism inevitable. The historical laws of capitalism's development, Marx insisted, "proved" the coming increasing misery of the working class and the concentration of wealth and capital into fewer and fewer hands, until society had been so polarized between a small handful of private owners of the means of production and an expanding poverty-stricken working class that revolutionary upheaval would sweep away the capitalist order and usher in a radical socialist transformation of the society.

The advocates of the welfare state, through most of this century, have believed Marx: Capitalism, if left alone, impoverishes the many and concentrates wealth into the hands of the few. Forestalling this has been the purpose of their reforms. *Social policy in the Western world, in other words, has been haunted by the ghost of Karl Marx. And in this crucial sense all welfare statist policies have rested on Marxian foundations.*

Having seen the future through Marx's eyes and been horrified by what they saw, the welfare statists claimed to know how to bring the power of the state to bear to correct capitalism's abuses and stop history from dragging society into the vortex of radical socialist revolution. Here emerges what Wilhelm Röpke once referred to as "the hubris of the intellect," the almost boastful self-confidence in a capacity for social engineering.[40] While the social reformers of the welfare state have claimed that theirs is the moderate alternative to comprehensive collectivism, their confidence in social engineering can be considered even more extreme than that of the radical socialists. Revolutionary socialists believed that the existing social order could not be incrementally repaired or improved. A leveling of all the institutions of society had to precede the remaking of society from the ground up.

The welfare statist social engineer has had confidence that he can tinker with the existing order to transform it and reshape it into forms more compatible with the virtues of socialism, while preserving particular features of the older order that he deems worthy of retention. He has believed that he knows how much industrial concentration is too much and what the optimal size of enterprises should be; he has believed that he knows what conditions of work and scale of wages amount to exploitation and are inconsistent with the healthy character of labor, and therefore he knows what those conditions of work and scale of wages should be; he has believed that he knows inhuman and excessively congested city life when he sees it, so he introduces urban planning and has engineered city development; he has believed that he knows at what point people, left to themselves in the marketplace, will fail to preserve sufficient wildlife and untouched nature areas, so he "modifies" property rights to enable the introduction of a planned environment that will be "naturally" balanced.

He has believed that he knows what family environment and private provision of education is incompatible with the fostering of well-balanced and "progressively" educated children for a better society tomorrow, so he has imposed compulsory public schooling, and designed a "rational" and "politically cor-

rect" curriculum reflecting what he knows to be the proper values and social norms of conduct that every human being
should have and practice.[41] He has believed that he knows
what is poverty and how to cure it, and has introduced income
transfers, provided public housing, created work-training programs and modified the definition of the meaning of a "family
unit," on the basis of which subsidies of various sorts are provided that are meant to engineer the emergence of "families"
more consistent with the social reformers' approved definition

And all the time the impression is created that fundamen-
tally everything is still the same. Private enterprise goes
about its business; people buy and sell in the marketplace;
workers pick and choose among jobs; private property is not
abolished; couples meet and marry, and parents still raise
their children. Yet it is no longer the same as it was before
the social engineer began his pragmatic and opportunististic
reforming of society. Beneath the case-by-case expediency of
social policy-making have been anti-capitalist, anti-freedom,
and anti-individualist premises. And guiding every turn of
the seemingly pragmatic pattern of welfare statist reform has
been a hidden compass directing the cumulative outcome
towards state-management, the regulated society and the
making of a new collectivist—now, "politically correct"—man
(or, in PC lingo, "person")![42]

The Bankruptcy of the Welfare State

Looking east across what had been the Iron Curtain, the failure of Soviet-style socialism is visible for all to see. Its destructive effect is evident to all except the blind or the self-deceiv-
ing. Socialism has been no less destructive in its welfare state
variation; only its form and degree are less easy to articulate
and identify. What many people feel is an uncomfortableness,
a sense that something is very wrong, that not every social policy has produced the desired effect, that somehow people and
society are not morally healthy and balanced.

In the former socialist East, it is possible to point to the principle that has failed—the total state and the centrally planned economy. But how does one put one's finger on the principle that has gone wrong in the Western welfare state when it has no articulated principle that guides it? A hundred years ago, the Socialists of the Chair of the German Historical School said, "The functions of the state are not susceptible of abstract, a priori deductions. Each proposal must be decided by the time and the conditions." The only principle is expediency. Where are the philosophical or political-economic theoretical principles from which one would critically evaluate and pass judgment upon the reasons for the bankruptcy of the welfare state? After a century of pragmatic reformist social engineering in both public education and the general culture, most people find it difficult even to comprehend the possibility of any Archimedean points from which to survey the damage and its causes.

This was lamented about already in the early 1950s by Wilhelm Röpke:

> If I were asked to say what appeared to me as one of the gravest features of our time I would answer: One of the worst things is that people do not seem to stop and think and ask themselves quietly what exactly they are doing....More and more people no longer know what it means to put first things first and to think in terms of the principles involved. Consequently, only a few still have a real philosophy which separates the essential from the accidental and which puts everything in its place....Confusion, loss of orientation and lack of philosophical insight are worse than ever, and so we are drifting on an uncharted sea. We are running after current events, instead of stopping to reach the solid grounds of principles and to ask ourselves seriously what have been the reasons why so much goodwill, energy, intelligence, time and money have been wasted or not given the result we had a right to expect.[43]

Marxism insisted that there were no permanent things; no invariable, essential aspects to human nature; no inherently appropriate institutional relationships that are most conducive to societal harmony and material prosperity, and that both our reason and historical experience could make known to us. What we take to be permanent things are really only transitory things at a particular moment of historical evolution, the Marxians insisted.

The Western world has been stripped of many of its principles concerning those permanent things. The only value judgment that we have been left with is that we are supposed to be nonjudgmental.[44] We may feel outrage, shock, disapproval or disappointment, but these are merely our "personal views." This, more than anything, is the moral bankruptcy of the welfare state. We are not permitted to ask: "What may be the 'rights of man?' What might be the legitimate, but limited functions of a government? When is a claimed entitlement nothing more than legalized plunder? Might there be moral standards, for personal conduct in private affairs as well as in the political arena, that our reason or our religion can guide us to have an understanding of, and that would not be the mere expediencies of the moment?" We are not even allowed to ask such questions in politically correct polite society.

At the end of his book, *Socialism,* Ludwig von Mises included a lengthy section on the consequences of the welfare state. He analyzed the effects from compulsory labor legislation, compulsory social insurance, trade unions, government subsidized unemployment insurance, socialization of selected industries, and fiscal policy and inflation. This section of his book is called "Destructionism." In it, Mises wrote, "Socialism is not in the least what it pretends to be . It is not the pioneer of a better and finer world, but the spoiler of what thousands of years of civilization have created. It does not build; it destroys. For destruction is the essence of it. It produces nothing, it only consumes what the social order based on private ownership in the means of production has created....Socialism must exhaust itself in the destruction of what already exists."[45]

Though not as visually dramatic as in Eastern Europe, socialism in the form of the welfare state has been destructive of our political, economic and cultural principles. It has been and is eating at us from the inside. And to a great extent its success has been due to the fact that after several generations of living under it, people don't even know it for what it is. The welfare state, for many, is a "just" and "caring" society. It is The American Way.[46]

It is time to call things by their real names. It is time to stop, and take the long view. It is time to reflect and try to rediscover some of the permanent principles that gave us the potential to be free and prosperous in the past, and which, if recaptured, might just possibly put us back on the road to a healthy civil society. If we do, then possibly all the victims of socialism in this century can finally put the destructive legacy of Karl Marx behind them.[47]

Notes

[1]Ludwig von Mises, *Socialism, An Economic and Sociological Analysis* [1922] (Indianapolis: Liberty Classics, [1951, revised ed.] 1981), 15.

[2]Even among the classical economists of the last century we can find the hope and belief in the possibility of remaking mankind, if only human beings could be enveloped by the right institutional environment. There was no greater and more respected figure among the English political economists of the mid-nineteenth century than John Stuart Mill. In his *Principles of Political Economy, with Some of Their Applications to Social Philosophy*, Mill says: "History bears witness to the success with which large bodies of human beings may be trained to feel the public interest their own. And no soil could be more favorable to the growth of such feeling than a communist association, since all the ambition and the bodily and mental activity, which are now exerted in the pursuit of separate and self-regarding interests, would require another sphere of employment and would naturally find it in the pursuit of the general benefit of the community. The same cause, so often assigned in explanation of the devotion of the Catholic priest or monk to the interest of his order—that he has no interest apart from it—would, under communism, attach the citizen to the community." On the errors in Mill's views concerning redistribution of wealth and socialism, see, Friedrich A. Hayek, "The Muddle of the Middle," in *Philosophical and Economic Foundations of Capitalism*, ed., Svetozar Pejovich (Lexington, Mass.: D.C. Heath, Co., 1983), 89–100.

[3]The next several paragraphs partly draw upon, Richard M. Ebeling, "National Health Insurance and the Welfare State," in Jacob G. Hornberger and Richard M. Ebeling, eds., *The Dangers of Socialized Medicine* (Fairfax: Future of Freedom Foundation, 1994), 25–37.

[4]See, Gustav Stolper, *The German Economy: 1870 to the Present* (London: Weidenfeld and Nicolson, [1940] revised ed., 1967), 43–46.

[5]William H. Dawson, *The Evolution of Modern Germany*, Vol. II (New York: Charles Scribner's Sons, 1914), 349.

[6]For a summary of the views of the German Historical School, or the "Socialists of the Chair," as they were also known, see, Émile de Laveleye, *The Socialism of Today* (London: Field and Tuer, The Leadenhall Press, 1890), 265–283; also, Eugen von Philippovich, "The Infusion of Socio-Political Ideas into the Literature of German Economics," *The American Journal of Sociology* (Sept., 1912), 145–199; John Kells Ingram, *A History of Political Economy* (London: A. & C. Black, Ltd., 1923), 192–232; Charles Gide and Charles Rist, *A History of Economic Doctrines: From the Time of the Physiocrats to the Present Day* (Boston: D. C. Heath and Co., 1928), 379–407; and Ludwig von Mises, *The Historical Setting of the Austrian School of Economics* (New Rochelle, N.Y.: Arlington House, 1969), 20–39.

[7]While these members of the German Historical School may have rejected the radical socialist agenda for a revolutionary transformation of the entire social order, their own agenda for a comprehensive system of welfare statist programs was entirely consistent with Marx's conception of one of the predominant functions of the state once the "bourgeois order" had been overthrown and replaced by the socialist state, which then would undertake its responsibilities during the transition leading to communism. See, Karl Marx, "Critique of the Gotha Program," [1875] in *The Marx-Engels Reader* ed. by Robert C. Tucker (New York: W.W. Norton & Co., Inc., 1972), 382–398, in which Marx argues that in the socialist state, before the workers are given the proceeds that are derived from their respective contributions to the overall output of the society, certain amounts first must be "deducted." Marx explains that these deductions from the total output of the society, before the workers receive the respective products of their labor, are to fund certain activities which will now be the responsibility of the socialist state to perform. Among these activities, Marx says, will be "reserve or insurance funds to provide against accidents, dislocations caused by natural calamities, etc....the common satisfaction of needs, such as schools, health services, etc....funds for those unable to work, etc., in short, for what is included under so-called official poor relief today." And as these welfare statist functions are taken on by the socialist state, now that capitalism has been abolished, "From the outset this part grows consider-

ably in comparison with present-day society and it grows in proportion as the new society develops," (385–386).

[8]William H. Dawson, *Bismarck and State Socialism* [1890] (New York: William Fertig, 1973), 2–4.

[9]See, Elmer Roberts, *Monarchical Socialism in Germany* (New York: Charles Scribner's Sons, 1913), 137–138: "Wagner, Schmoller, Schoenberg, Schaeffle, and others, originating and supporting principles of monarchical socialism, took the middle course between the extreme socialism of Lassalle, Marx, and Rodbertus, which would have...government do everything, and the individualism of the Manchester school, limiting the powers of government to the simplest functions of administration and defense. The endeavor of German statesmanship has been to hold to everything in existing social arrangements necessary to produce individuality in the higher orders, and yet to intervene in education, sanitation, sick, accident and old-age insurance, the physical training of youth in the army, and to participate in transportation, forestry, mining, farming, and industrial enterprises, designing thus to raise the lower orders mentally, physically, and economically, so that they too become worthier individuals, adding to the power of the state and the monarchy. The intervention of the government is to be determined by expediency. The government, guided by circumstances, is ready either to take part in phases of economic life or to let individualism remain in control of them." See, also, Ralph H. Bowen, *German Theories of the Corporative State, with Special Reference to the Period, 1870–1919* (New York: Russell & Russell, [1947] 1971), Ch. IV on "Monarchical Socialism," 119–159.

[10]Frederic C. Howe, *Socialized Germany* (New York: Charles Scribner's Sons, 1915), 162.

[11]Ibid., 83–85.

[12]Ibid., 82–83; also, Dawson, *Bismarck and State Socialism*, 4–6: "No department of economic activity should on principle be closed to the state; whether it should or not participate, side by side, with private enterprise, is a matter of expediency and public interest....It is evident that the principles of state intervention in economic affairs and state care and protection for the poorer classes being posited, it is difficult to say how far these principles should be carried. The state socialists say that this must be determined by expediency, and by circumstances of time and place....The bounds of the state's functions have not, like the earth's foundations, been fixed from of old, that they should not be removed. The jurisdiction of government is a matter not of principle but of expediency."

[13]Eugen von Philippovich, "The Verein für Sozialpolitik," *Quarterly Journal of Economics* (January, 1891), 227–228.

[14]Joseph A. Schumpeter, *History of Economic Analysis* (New York: Oxford University Press, 1954), 864, explains that a sizable number of American economists, "not finding in the [U.S.] what they wanted, continued to rely on European ideas and methods though no longer exclusively English ones—the pilgrimage to Germany, in particular, became for those who could afford it almost a regular incident of their career, something like the Cavalier's tour of old;" see, also, Charles F. Thwing, *The American and the German University* (New York: Macmillan and Co., 1928); Jergen Herbst, *The German Historical School in American Scholarship* (Ithaca: Cornell University Press, 1965); and, Joseph Dorfman, "The Role of the German Historical School in American Economic Thought," *American Economic Review* (May, 1955), 17–28.

[15]Among them were John Bates Clark, Edwin Seligman and Henry Seager of Columbia University; Richard T. Ely of the University of Wisconsin; Arthur Twining Hadley, president of Yale University; Frank W. Taussig of Harvard University; Albion Small of the University of Chicago; Edmund J. James, president of the University of Illinois; Joseph French Johnson of New York University; Simon N. Patten of the University of Pennsylvania; Frank A. Fetter of Princeton University; Wesley C. Mitchell of the National Bureau of Economic Research; and Herbert J. Davenport of Cornell University. See, Frank A. Fetter, "The Economists and the Public," *American Economic Review* (March, 1925), 13–26, for a flavor of "the new thinking" among these German-trained American economists, and their disapproval of the "older" economists and businessmen who emphasized limited government involvement in market affairs.

[16]Wesley C. Mitchell, *Types of Economic Theory*, Vol. II (New York: Augustus M. Kelley, 1969), 233–234.

[17]See, Arthur A. Ekirch, Jr., *Progressivism in America* (New York: New Viewpoints, 1974), 19–33.

[18]J. Laurence Laughlin, *The Elements of Political Economy, with Some Applications to Questions of the Day* (New York: American Book Co., 1887), 265 & 268; emphasis in the original. See, also, Laughlin's *Latter-Day Problems*, (New York: Charles Scribner's Sons, [1907] revised edition, 1917), in which he challenged the socialist and welfare statist arguments of his younger colleagues infused with those paternalistic German ideas. Laughlin's lonely voice was joined by his Harvard University colleague, Thomas Nixon Carver, *Essays in Social Justice* (Cambridge: Cambridge University Press, 1915) and, Carver, "Liberalism at Harvard," *Harvard Graduate's Magazine* (March, 1919), 278–288; these new paternalistic and redistributive ideas were already criticized even earlier with great cogency by William Graham Sumner, *What Social Classes Owe to Each Other* [1883] (Caldwell, Idaho: Caxton Printers, Ltd., 1966).

[19]Henry Seager, "Economics at Berlin and Vienna," *Journal of Political Economy* (March, 1893), 236–262, reprinted in, Seager, *Labor and Other Economic Essays*, ed. by Charles A. Gulick, Jr. (Freeport, N.Y.: Books for Libraries [1931] 1968), 1–29.

[20]Henry Seager, *Principles of Economics* (New York: Henry Holt and Co., 1913), 536–612; similar analyses and conclusions, also drawing upon the German experience, can be found in Edwin R. A. Seligman, *Principles of Economics* (New York: Longmans, Green, and Co., 1914), 643–693; Frank A. Fetter, *Modern Economic Problems* (New York: Century Co., 1916), 314–364; though often embraced as an Austrian economist because of his important contributions to the theory of value, rent, capital and interest, Frank Fetter was a proponent of welfare statist legislation, arguing that in the areas of accident, sickness, old-age and unemployment insurance: "The state, through the public insurance office, must ultimately be the sole agency for insurance....There should be a unification of various kinds of insurance in one general plan and under one general administration for the whole state," (362); Richard T. Ely, *Outlines of Economics* (New York: Macmillan Co., 1919), 444–492 & 577–595; even so careful a scholar as Frank Taussig of Harvard University, who in reviewing the various schemes for state-managed social insurance programs pointed out many of their potential perverse incentives and moral hazards, and explained the superiority of many private-sector alternatives as they had been administered in both the United States and Great Britain, had nothing but praise for the German welfare statist system. Indeed, he went as far as to say, "Hardly another country possesses the staff of trained public servants needed for planning and administering so vast a machinery for social reform; and the Germans are justly proud of what they have here achieved." See, Frank W. Taussig, *Principles of Economics*, Vol. II (New York: Macmillan Co., 1915), 331.

[21]Henry Seager, *Principles of Economics*, 622–623.

[22]Cf., Richard M. Ebeling, "Liberalism and Collectivism in the Twentieth Century," in *The End of "Isms"? Reflections on the Fate of Ideological Politics after Communism's Collapse*, ed., Aleksandras Shtromas (Cambridge: Blackwell Publishers, 1994), 69–84.

[23]Cf., Richard M. Ebeling, "How Economics Became the Dismal Science," in *Economic Education: What Should We Learn About the Free Market?* ed., Richard M. Ebeling, Champions of Freedom Series, Vol. 22 (Hillsdale: Hillsdale College Press, 1994), 51–81.

[24]Richard T. Ely, *Socialism: An Examination of Its Nature, Its Strengths and Its Weaknesses, with Suggestions for Social Reform* (New York: Thomas Y. Crowell & Co., 1895), 352–354.

[25]See, James Bovard, *Lost Rights: The Destruction of American Liberties* (New

York: St. Martin's Press, 1994) for numerous specific examples and case-studies of such intrusions and controls of the sort mentioned in the next several paragraphs.

26See, Richard A. Epstein, *Takings: Private Property and the Power of Eminent Domain* (Cambridge: Harvard University Press, 1985); Epstein, *Bargaining with the State* (Princeton: Princeton University Press, 1993); Mark L. Pollot, *Grand Theft and Petit Larceny: Property Rights in America* (San Francisco: Pacific Research Institute for Public Policy, 1993).

27See, Nathan Glazer, *Affirmative Action: Ethnic Inequality and Public Policy* (New York: Basic Books, 1975); Terry Eastland and William J. Bennett, *Counting by Race: Equality from the Founding Fathers to* Bakke *and* Weber (New York: Basic Books, 1979); Walter E. Block and Michael A. Walker, ed., *Discrimination, Affirmative Action, and Equal Opportunity* (Vancouver, B.C.: Fraser Institute, 1982); Walter Williams, *The State Against Blacks* (New York: McGraw-Hill Book Co., 1982); Thomas Sowell, *Civil Rights: Rhetoric or Reality?* (New York: William Morrow and Co., 1984); Nicholas Capaldi, *Out of Order: Affirmative Action and the Crisis of Doctrinaire Liberalism* (Buffalo; N.Y.: Prometheus Books, 1985); Clint Bolick, *Changing Course: Civil Rights at the Crossroads* (New Brunswick, N.J.: Transaction Books, 1988); Bolick, *Unfinished Business: A Civil Rights Strategy for America's Third Century* (San Francisco: Pacific Research Institute for Public Policy, 1990); Herman Belz, *Equality Transformed: A Quarter-Century of Affirmative Action* (New Brunswick, N.J.: Transaction Books, 1991); and Richard A. Epstein, *Forbidden Grounds: The Case Against Employment Discrimination Laws* (Cambridge: Harvard University Press, 1992).

28Martin Anderson, *Welfare: The Political Economy of Welfare Reform in the United States* (Stanford: Hoover Institution Press, 1978); Brigitte Berger and Peter L. Berger, *The War Over the Family: Capturing the Middle Ground* (Garden City, N.Y.: Anchor Press/Doubleday, 1983); Charles Murray, *Losing Ground: American Social Policy, 1950–1980* (New York: Basic Books, 1984); Charles Murray, *The Emerging British Underclass* (London: Institute of Economic Affairs, 1990) and *Underclass: The Crisis Deepens* (London: Institute of Economic Affairs, 1994); Patricia Morgan *Farewell to the Family? Public Policy and Family Breakdown in Britain and the USA* (London: Institute of Economic Affairs, 1995); on the general paternalistic character of the welfare state, and its ideological and philosophical premises, see, Jack D. Douglas, *The Myth of the Welfare State* (New Brunswick, N.J.: Transaction Books, 1989).

29See, Terry L. Anderson and Peter J. Hill, *The Birth of the Transfer Society* (Stanford: Hoover Institution, 1980).

30Vilfredo Pareto, "Socialism and Freedom," [1891] in *The Other Pareto*, ed., Placido Bucolo (New York: St. Martin's Press, 1980), 44 & 46–47.

[31]The next several paragraphs partly draw upon, Richard M. Ebeling, "Democratized Privilege: The New Mercantilism," *Freedom Daily* (Feb., 1991), 6–10, and "Producer Interests vs. The Public Interest: The Origin of Democratized Privilege," *Freedom Daily* (March, 1991), 6–10.

[32]Adam Smith, *The Wealth of Nations* [1776] (New York: Modern Library, 1937) Book I, Chapter I, 5.

[33]See, on the role of private property as a protector of individual liberty in a system of division of labor, James M. Buchanan, *Property as a Guarantor of Liberty* (Brookfield, Vt.: Edward Elgar Publishing Co., 1993).

[34]Wilhelm Röpke, *The Social Crises of Our Time* [1942] (Chicago: University of Chicago Press, 1950), 129; also, see, Philip Wicksteed, *The Common Sense of Political Economy*, Vol. I [1910] (London: Routledge & Kegan Paul, Ltd., 1933), 349–357; and Oskar Morgenstern, *The Limits of Economics* [1934] (London: William Hodge and Co., Ltd., 1937), Ch. IV on, "The Distribution Effects of Economic Policy," 29–46. In the last thirty years, the economic analysis of the incentives for and financial costs to the society from the process of special interest lobbying for governmental privileges and subsidies—politically-derived profits, rather than market-derived profits—has come to be called "rent-seeking" behavior; see, James M. Buchanan, Robert D. Tollison and Gordon Tullock, eds., *Toward a Theory of the Rent-Seeking Society* (College Station: Texas A &M University Press, 1980); Robert B. Ekelund and Robert D. Tollison, *Mercantilism as a Rent-Seeking Society: Economic Regulation in Historical Perspective* (College Station: Texas A & M University Press, 1981); Robert D. Tollison, "Rent-Seeking: A Survey," *Kyklos* (Vol. 35, No. 4, 1982), 575–692; David C. Collander, ed., *Neoclassical Political Economy: The Analysis of Rent-Seeking and DUP Activities* (Cambridge: Ballinger Publishing Co., 1984); Gordon Tullock, *The Economics of Special Privilege and Rent-Seeking* (Boston: Kluwer Academic Press, 1989); Richard E. Wagner, *To Promote the General Welfare: Market Processes vs. Political Transfers* (San Francisco: Pacific Research Institute for Public Policy, 1989); and Gordon Tullock, *Rent-Seeking* (Brookfield, Vt.: Edward Elgar Publishing Co., 1993).

[35]On the meaning of the nomenklatura and its political power and position in the former Soviet economic system, see, Richard M. Ebeling, "Introduction" and "The Inevitability of Capitalism and the Problems of Privatizing the Socialist Economy," in *Can Capitalism Cope? Free Market Reform in the Post-Communist World*, ed., Richard M. Ebeling, Champions of Freedom Series, Vol. 21 (Hillsdale: Hillsdale College Press, 1994), 8–9 & 34–38.

[36]On the different views of the behaviorial characteristics of man, as often presented by economists, political scientists, and sociologists, respectively, see, Karl Brunner and William H. Meckling, "The Perception of Man and the Conception of Government," *Journal of Money, Credit and Banking*

(Feb., 1977), Part I, 70–85; and Karl Brunner, "The Perceptions of Man and the Conception of Society: Two Approaches to Understanding Society," *Economic Inquiry* (July, 1987), 367–388.

[37]Ludwig von Mises, "The Myth of the Failure of Capitalism," [1932] in *The Clash of Group Interests and Other Essays*, ed., Richard M. Ebeling (New York: Center for Libertarian Studies, 1978), 16–17.

[38]Richard T. Ely, *Socialism: An Examination of Its Nature, Its Strengths and Its Weaknesses, with Suggestions for Social Reform*, 256.

[39]Ibid., 355–359.

[40]Wilhelm Röpke, *Civitas Humana: A Humane Order of Society* [1944] (London: William Hodge and Co., Ltd., 1948), 43–56.

[41]See, Sheldon Richman, *Separating School and State: How to Liberate America's Families* (Fairfax: Future of Freedom Foundation, 1994).

[42]Cf., Friedrich A. Hayek, *Law, Legislation and Liberty*, Vol. I: "Rules and Order" (Chicago: University of Chicago Press, 1973), Ch. 3 on "Principles and Expediency," 55–71.

[43]Wilhelm Röpke, "The Problem of Economic Order," [1951] in *Two Essays by Wilhelm Röpke*, ed., Johannes Overbeck (Lanham, MD: University Press of America, 1987), 1–2.

[44]In opposition to this view, for a discussion on the role of value judgments in thinking about and debating questions concerning social theory and social policy, see, Wilhelm Röpke, "A Value Judgment on Value Judgments," *Revue de la Faculte des Sciences Economique d'Istabul* (Vol. III, No. 1–2, 1942), 1–19.

[45]Ludwig von Mises, *Socialism*, 458.

[46]On some of the ideas and events in twentieth-century American history that have helped undermine the traditional American system and the values underlying it, see, Robert Nisbet, *The Present Age: Progress and Anarchy in Modern America* (New York: Harper and Row, 1988).

[47]In Richard M. Ebeling, "How Economics Became the Dismal Science," op. cit., I have tried to explain some of the universals of the human condition, as understood by the classical economists, that are essential to and can help secure a free and prosperous society. And in Richard M. Ebeling, "The Significance of Austrian Economics in Twentieth-Century Economic Thought," in *Austrian Economics: Perspectives on the Past and Prospects for the Future*, ed., Richard M. Ebeling, Champions of Freedom Series, Vol. 17 (Hillsdale: Hillsdale College Press, 1990), 1–40, I have attempted to outline the insights of the Austrian economists concerning the nature of human action, the market economy, and the spontaneous social order that are the foundation for a free and prosperous society.

Charles Murray

Help the Poor: Abolish Welfare*

In the 1992 campaign, Bill Clinton's television ad promising to "end welfare as we know it" was one of his best vote-getters, so effective that it was the first choice for a heavy media buy in closely contested states at the end of the campaign. This should come as no surprise. No American social program has been so unpopular, so consistently or so long, as welfare. But why?

What Is Wrong with Welfare?

What is wrong with welfare that evokes such a widespread urge to "do something about it"? Two obvious candidates are size and cost. Bill Clinton campaigned during a surging increase in the welfare rolls. By the end of his first year in office, more than fourteen million people would be enrolled in Aid to Families with Dependent Children (AFDC), representing more than 7 percent of American families and two million more recipients than had been on the rolls in 1989.

With so many working-aged people being supported by government, the amounts of money involved have mounted

---

*Also published as "What to Do About Welfare," *Commentary* (December 1994), 26–34.

accordingly. But, as with so many other questions involving welfare, there is no uncontroversial answer as to exactly how much, because few can agree about where the definition of "welfare" begins and ends.

In 1990, before the most recent increase in the rolls had gotten well under way, figures cited by various parties in the welfare debate ranged from $21 billion to $210 billion. The lower figure, used by those who claim that welfare is really a piddling part of the budget, represents just AFDC. But no serious student of the issue denies that Medicaid, food stamps, and public housing are also part of welfare. That brings the total to $129 billion. But this number covers only part of the array of programs for low-income families. The upper-end figure of $210 billion is the bottom line for the Congressional Research Service's report of state and federal expenditures on "cash and noncash benefits for persons with limited income" in 1990. Of that, $152 billion came from the federal government.

Two hundred and ten billion dollars works out to $6,270 for every man, woman, and child under the poverty line in 1990, only a few hundred dollars less than the official poverty threshold ($6,270 for a single unrelated individual in 1990). Statements such as "We could eliminate poverty tomorrow if we just gave the money we're already spending directly to poor people" may be oversimplified, but they are not so far off the mark either.

One approach to the topic of "what to do about welfare" could thus reasonably involve ways to reduce expenditures. Yet, though complaints about wasting money on welfare loafers are commonly heard, and though the country truly does spend a lot of money on welfare, it is not obvious that money is really the problem. Suppose that for $210 billion we were buying peaceful neighborhoods and happy, healthy children in our low-income neighborhoods. Who would say that the nation could not afford it? Money may well become a decisive issue as the dependent population continues to grow, but is has not yet.

Instead, I will proceed from the assumption that the main source of the nationwide desire to do something about welfare is grounded in concerns about what welfare is doing to the health of the society. Judging from all that can be found in the press, on talk shows, and in the technical literature, an unusually broad consensus embracing just about everyone except the hard-core Left now accepts that something has gone drastically wrong with the family, that the breakdown is disproportionately found in poor neighborhoods, and that the welfare system is deeply implicated.

Different people put different emphases on just what has gone wrong. There are so many choices. In many welfare families, no one has ever held a regular job. This is bad for the taxpayer who supports such families, bad for the women who are trapped into poverty, and most portentously in the long run, bad for children who need to be socialized to the world of work. In many welfare families, the mother works, but only sporadically and surreptitiously in the illegal economy. The welfare system becomes an instrument for teaching her children all the wrong lessons about how to get along in life.

In the vast majority of welfare homes, there is no biological father in the house. In many, there has never been a father. The male figure in the home is instead likely to consist of a series of boyfriends who do not act as fathers but as abusive interlopers.

These circumstances are damaging to children in so many ways that to list them individually would be to trivialize them. On this issue, the intellectual conventional wisdom has changed remarkably in just the last few years. The visible turning point was Barbara Dafoe Whitehead's 1993 *Atlantic* article, "Dan Quayle Was Right," but the groundwork had been laid in the technical journals in preceding years, as more and more scholars concluded that single parenthood was bad for children independently of poverty and other markers of socioeconomic disadvantage.

Statistically, measures of child well-being tend to order families by their structure: conditions are best for children in intact families, next best for children of divorce (it does not seem to help if the custodial parent remarries), and worst for children born out of wedlock (even if the woman later marries another man). This ordering applies to a wide variety of outcomes, from emotional development to school performance to delinquency to family formation in the next generation.

But evidence accumulated so far tells only part of the story. Families that have been on welfare for long periods of time are overwhelmingly concentrated in communities where many other welfare families live. While it is unfortunate when a child must grow up in a family without a father, it is a disaster when a generation of children—especially a generation of male children—grows up in a neighborhood without fathers. The proof of this is before our eyes in the black inner city, where the young men reaching twenty in 1994 came of age in neighborhoods in which about half the children were born out of wedlock. Social science is only beginning to calibrate the extent and nature of the "neighborhood effects" that compound the problems associated with illegitimacy.

If these results were confined to the inner cities of our major cities, the effects on American society would still be grim enough. A look at the national mood about crime shows how a problem that is still localized (as the most severe crime rates still are, impressions notwithstanding) can nonetheless impinge on American life as a whole. But there is no reason to think that the effects will remain within the black inner city. The white illegitimacy ratio, which stood at 22 percent for all whites in 1991, is approaching the 50-percent mark in a number of working-class American cities. There is no good reason to assume that white communities with extremely high illegitimacy rations will escape the effects of an unsocialized new generation.

These observations have led me to conclude that illegitimacy is the central social problem of our time, and that its spread threatens the underpinning of a free society. We cannot have a free society, by this reasoning, unless the great majority of young people come of age having internalized norms of self-restraint, self-reliance, and commitment to a civic order, and receive an upbringing that prepares them to transmit these same values to their children. We cannot achieve that kind of socialization without fathers playing a father's role in the great majority of homes where children grow up.

For those who accept this pessimistic reasoning, extreme measures to change the welfare system are justified; for those who still consider illegitimacy to be one problem among many, more incremental reforms seem called for. Put broadly, four types of welfare reform are being considered in various combinations: workfare, the substitution of work for welfare; penalties for fathers; and the complete abolition of welfare.

Workfare

Workfare refers to a variety of reforms that would make welfare beneficiaries show up at some sort of job, usually a public-service one, or lose their benefits. Softer versions of workfare call upon welfare recipients to attend job-training programs or risk losing their benefits. Offshoots include such things as "learnfare," in which mothers lose part or all of their benefits if their children drop out of school.

The rationale for workfare that resonates with the voters is, roughly, "Make them do something for the money we're giving them." Many also hope that the prospect of having to work for benefits will either deter young women from having babies in the first place or induce them to find real jobs on their own and leave welfare.

An additional intellectual rationale has been advanced by Lawrence Mead, a political scientist at New York University, who argues that what welfare recipients really lack is the ability to cope with the routines of ordinary life. Surveys show that they share the same aspirations as people in mainstream society, Mead says, but their lives are so chaotic and their discipline so ill-formed that the government must provide the framework that has been missing in their own lives.

Workfare is not an untried idea. Local attempts to force women to work for welfare have been made off and on in scattered jurisdictions for decades. The 1988 welfare-reform bill put the federal government's imprimatur on such programs. The evaluation reports now add up to a fair-sized library, and they tell a consistent story. Participants in training and work programs usually have higher mean earnings than persons in the control groups. But these mean differences amount to hundreds of dollars per year, not thousands. The effects on long-term employment are small. The most successful programs tend to be located in small cities and rural areas rather than large cities.

A few exceptions to these generalizations are noteworthy. A program in Riverside, California, showed dramatic early results, apparently because of an energetic, decisive administrator who was given extraordinary freedom to define work rules, replace staff who did not perform, and enforce sanctions against welfare recipients who did not cooperate. If anyone can figure out how to duplicate these conditions nationwide, workfare might be able to produce much larger effects than shown in the typical evaluation.

As far as I know, no one has ever documented a deterrent effect for workfare. But evidence indicates that many welfare recipients, sometimes a significant portion of the total caseload, will drop out of a welfare program if a strictly enforced work requirement is installed.

The Substitution of Work for Welfare

In 1986, the social critic Mickey Kaus proposed an alternative to workfare that would scrap the existing welfare system and replace it with public-service jobs at the minimum wage.

The government would provide medical care and child care for preschool children, but otherwise the woman would be on her own. If she showed up at one of the local job sites and worked, she would get a paycheck at the end of the week. If she chose not to work, that would be her business.

Kaus's proposal, which he subsequently elaborated in his book, *The End of Equality*, has much to recommend it. Workfare programs break down because of built-in contradictions. Welfare bureaucracies do not function well as employers. They have no incentives to reduce their caseloads and no incentives to make welfare recipients behave as real employees. Trying to enforce sanctions against uncooperative cases tends to become a long and tedious process. The Kaus system asks only that the government recreate a WPA-style agency for administering public-service jobs—something that the government did successfully in the 1930s.

Whether the government could do as much again is open to question. The typical WPA male worker in the 1930s came to the program with a set of motivations much different from those of the typical AFDC mother in the 1990s. Yet it seems plausible to me that the Kaus system would not only achieve substantial effects on work behavior among AFDC mothers but also have a substantial deterrent effect.

The program's cost, which Kaus himself set at $43 billion to $59 billion for national implementation, might not be as large as expected. Since we know that large proportions of the caseload have taken themselves off the rolls when a strict work requirement was imposed, we could expect a similarly large drop if the Kaus plan were implemented. And while it is difficult to imagine the federal government adopting a scrap-welfare-for-work proposal with the pristine purity necessary to make it succeed, it is possible to imagine a state doing so, if states were given the option of folding all the money currently spent on AFDC, food stamps, and public housing into a public-service jobs program.

Penalties for Fathers

Enforcement of child support among unmarried fathers is one of the most popular reforms under consideration, not least because it gives people a chance to say the right things about the responsibilities of the male. Like workfare, enforcement of child support is an old idea. Toughly worded laws are already on the books requiring child support, and the federal government is spending about $2 billion a year on the Child Support Enforcement program originated in 1975.

Despite these efforts, paternity is not established for about two-thirds of illegitimate births. The failure rate is so high partly because of poor enforcement, but mainly because the law asks so little of the unwed mother. The government has leverage only when she wants to qualify for AFDC benefits. For this, she is required merely to cooperate in identifying the father, a condition that can be satisfied by giving the name of a man whose whereabouts are unknown or even by her earnest statement that she does not know who the father is.

The proposed reform with the most teeth is to withhold all AFDC benefits unless the father is actually identified and located. Would such a threat help control the behavior of males? Perhaps—if the father had a job in the above-ground economy, if the state had in place methods of garnishing his wages, and if the state were able summarily to jail fathers who failed to meet their obligations.

Yet to list these conditions is to expose the reasons not to expect much from reforms of child support. Many unwed fathers have no visible means of support, and an even higher proportion will flee into that category, or disappear entirely, if child-support enforcement is tightened.

Would such measures nonetheless "send the right signals" about the responsibilities of men for their children? Many think so; I am a holdout. The alternative "right signal" is to tell young women from the outset—from childhood—that they had better choose the father of their babies very carefully, because it is next to impossible for anyone, including the state, to force a man to take on the responsibilities of fatherhood.

The Complete Abolition of Welfare

This brings us to the fourth option, scrapping welfare altogether, a proposal which I have advocated for some years. I am under no illusions that Congress is about to pass such a plan nationally. But, as with the Kaus plan, a state can do what the federal government cannot. And it is conceivable that Congress will pass reforms permitting the states wide discretion in restructuring the way they spend their welfare budgets.

These goals presume that ending welfare will have a drastic effect on behavior. One must ask whether there is good reason to believe that it will.

One way of approaching the question is to ask whether welfare causes illegitimacy in the first place. I have written two reviews of this debate in the past two years—one long and technical, the other shorter and nontechnical—and will not try to cover all of the ground here.[1] These are the highlights plus a few new points:

Academics have focused almost exclusively on comparisons of illegitimacy based on the differences in welfare payments across states. It is now generally, if reluctantly, acknowledged by these scholars that the generosity of welfare benefits has a relationship to extramarital fertility among whites. More recent work is showing that a relationship exists among blacks as well. The size of the effect for whites seems to be in the region of a 5 percent change in extramarital fertility for a 10 percent change in benefits, with some of the estimates substantially larger than that.

This effect is called small by those unhappy to admit that welfare has any relationship at all to extramarital fertility. I treat the fact that *any* effect has been found as I would treat favorable testimony from a hostile witness—the analyses have generally consisted of regression equations with a multitude of independent variables, making it as hard as possible to show an independent effect for AFDC. A broader observation about these studies is that trying to analyze the relationship of welfare to illegitimacy by examining cross-state variation in AFDC benefits has a number of serious methodological problems that are bound to limit the magnitude of the effect that AFDC is permitted to show. I have been pointing to such problems in print for many years. So far as I know, none of the analyses using cross-state benefits has even acknowledged the existence of these technical problems, much less tried to deal with them.

Last summer, 76 social scientists signed a statement saying that the relationship of welfare to illegitimacy was small. When I replied that the very studies they had in mind were consistent with something in the neighborhood of a 50-percent drop in white illegitimacy if welfare were eliminated, there were cries of outrage—but not because my statement was technically inaccurate. It was a straightforward extrapolation of the 5 percent (or more) change in white fertility per 10 percent change in welfare benefits that has been found in recent research.

I should add that I do not place much faith in such linear extrapolations in this case. Indeed, I argue from other evidence that the effects would most likely steepen as the reductions in welfare approached 100 percent. But this is speculative—no one has any empirical way to estimate how the curve might be shaped.

Meanwhile, two characteristics of illegitimate births imply a stronger relationship to welfare than that indicated by the cross-state analyses.

The first of these characteristics is that the illegitimate birth rate has been increasing while the legitimate birth rate has been decreasing. The *rate* in this case refers to the production of babies per unit of population, in contrast to the more commonly used statistic, the illegitimacy *ratio*, representing the proportion of live births that are extramarital.

The logic goes like this: Birth rates are driven by broad his-

toric forces that are so powerful and so consistent that they
have applied everywhere in the West. Put simply, birth rates fall
wherever women have an option to do something besides have
babies. The options are brought about by better medical care
(so more babies survive to adulthood), increased wealth and
educational opportunities, and the opening of careers to
women. Improved technology for birth control and access to
abortion facilitate the effects of these forces.

Thanks to all this, among both blacks and whites in America, the number of legitimate babies per unit of population
has been falling steeply. But during this same period, concentrated in the post-1960s, the number of illegitimate
babies per unit of population has been rising. In other
words, something is increasing the production of one kind
of baby (that born to single women) at the same time that
the production of the other kind of baby (that born to married women) is dropping.

The scholars who say that welfare cannot be an important
cause of the breakdown of marriage and the encouragement
of illegitimacy have yet to offer an explanation of what this mysterious something might be. The existence of a welfare system
that pays single women to have babies meets the test of parsimony.

Perhaps, however, the "mysterious something" is the lack of
these new options for disadvantaged women. But why specify
single disadvantaged women? That brings us to one of the most
provocative features of illegitimacy: its relationship to
poverty—not poverty after the baby is born, but before. It is
one of the stronger reasons for believing that the welfare system is implicated in the production of illegitimate babies.

Begin with young single women from affluent families or
women in high-paying jobs. For them, the welfare system is
obviously irrelevant. They are restrained from having babies
out of wedlock by moral considerations, by fear of the social
penalties (both of which still exist, though weakened, in middle-class circles), by a concern that the child have a father

around the house, and because having a baby would interfere with their plans for the future.

In most of the poorest communities, having a baby out of wedlock is no longer subject to social stigma, nor do moral considerations still appear to carry much weight. But the welfare system is very much a part of the picture. For a poor young woman, the welfare system is highly relevant to her future if she has a child, easing the short-term economic penalties that might ordinarily restrain her childbearing. The poorer she is, the more attractive the welfare package, and the more likely that she will think herself enabled by it to have a baby.

The implication of this logic is that illegitimate births will be concentrated among poor young women—and they are. This may be inferred from the information about family income from the Bureau of the Census data, showing that in 1992, women with incomes of less than $20,000 contributed 73 percent of all illegitimate babies, while women with incomes above $75,000 contributed just 2 percent.

But these data are imprecise, because income may have fallen after the baby was born (and the woman had to quit work, for example). The logic linking welfare to illegitimacy specifically refers to women who are poor before the baby is born. For data on this point, I turn to one of the best available bases, the National Longitudinal Survey of Young (NLSY),[2] and ask: Of women of all races who were below the poverty line in the year prior to giving birth, how many of their children were born out of wedlock? The answer is 56 percent. Among women who were anywhere above the poverty line, only 11 percent of babies were born out of wedlock.

Why should illegitimate births be so much more likely to occur among women who are already poor? The common argument that young women with few prospects "want something to love" may be true, but it has no answer to the obvious rejoinder, that single poor young women in the years before the welfare system began probably wanted something to love as well, and yet the vast majority of them nonetheless made sure they were married before bearing a child. Other things being equal, poor single young women face the most daunting prospects if they have a baby without a man to help take care of it, and that reality used to govern the behavior of such young women. Of course, the sexual revolution has changed the behavior of young women at all levels of society, but why has it produced babies predominantly in just one economic class?

Once again, an answer based on a welfare system that offers incentives only to poor women meets the test of parsimony. Once again, the scholarly literature has yet to offer an alternative explanation, or even to acknowledge that an alternative explanation is called for.

There is one additional characteristic of women who are at most risk of giving birth to children out of wedlock: they generally have low intelligence. This point is new to the welfare debate. Richard Herrnstein and I discuss it at length in *The Bell Curve*, again using the National Longitudinal Survey of Young, which administered a high-quality cognitive test to its subjects when the study began. The chances that a poor young woman's baby would be born out of wedlock were 68 percent if she had an IQ of 85, but only 26 percent if she had an IQ of 115.

Lest it be thought that this result is conflated with racial complications, it should be noted that the relationship held among whites as powerfully as among the population as a whole. Lest it be thought that the result is conflated with the opportunity that smart women have to go to college, it should also be noted that the relationship holds as powerfully among women who never got beyond high school as it does for the population as a whole. Lest it be thought that this is a reflection of socioeconomic background, the independent importance of IQ is still great after holding socioeconomic status constant. Conversely, the independent importance of socioeconomic background after holding the effects of IQ constant is severely attenuated.

Summarizing the overall picture: Women in the NLSY (in

their mid-twenties to early thirties when this observation applies) who remained childless or had babies within marriage had a mean IQ of 102. Those who had an illegitimate baby but never went on welfare had a mean IQ of 93. Those who went on welfare but did not become chronically dependent on welfare had a mean IQ of 89. Those who became chronic welfare recipients had a mean IQ of 85.

Now back to the first and most crucial goal of welfare reform, that it drastically reduce the number of children conceived by unmarried women. In trying to develop methods for accomplishing this goal, we know from the outset that both sex and the cuddliness of babies are going to continue to exert their powerful attractions. We know that decisions about whether to have sex and whether to use birth control are not usually made in moments of calm reflection. Therefore, any reform must somehow generate a situation in which a young woman, despite not being calm and reflective, and often despite not being very bright, is so scared at the prospect of getting pregnant that she will not have intercourse, or will take care not to get pregnant if she does.

This means that the welfare reform will have accomplished one of two things. Either the change has been so big, so immediate, and so punishing that even a young, poor, and not very smart girl has been affected by it; or else the change has directly motivated people around that young woman to take an active role in urging her not to have the baby.

Bill Clinton's program, based on the threat of "two years and out, if you've had a reasonable chance at job training and a reasonable chance to find a job," is not calculated to meet this criterion. Two years is an eternity to a young girl. The neighborhood is filled with single women who have been on welfare for ages and have not gotten thrown off. Is a sixteen-year-old going to believe that she will really be cut off welfare two years down the road, or will she believe the daily evidence around her?

Other commonly urged recommendations—sex education, counseling, and the like—are going to be just as futile. A major change in the behavior of young women and the adults in their lives will occur only when the prospect of having a child out of wedlock is once again so immediately, tangibly punishing that it overrides everything else—the importuning of the male, the desire for sex, the thoughtlessness of the moment, the anticipated cuddliness of the baby. Such a change will take place only when young people have had it drummed into their heads from their earliest memories that having a baby without a husband entails awful consequences. Subtle moral reasoning is not the response that works. "My father would kill me" is the kind of response that works.

From time immemorial, fathers and mothers raised the vast majority of their daughters, bright ones and dull ones, to understand these lessons. Somehow, in the last half-century, they began to lose their capacity to do so—curiously, just as social-welfare benefits for single women expanded. I want to press the argument that the overriding threat, short-term and tangible, which once sustained low illegitimacy ratios was the economic burden that the single woman presented to her parents and to the community. I do not mean to deny the many ways in which non-economic social stigma played a role or to minimize the importance of religious belief, but I would argue that much of their force was underwritten by economics.

At this point, we reach a question that cannot be answered by more social-science research but only by experience: If welfare were to be abolished in the late twentieth century, would a revival of the economic threat be enough to drive down illegitimacy? Or do we need a contemporaneous revival of the moral sanctions against illegitimacy to make the economic penalties work? The good news is that the two forces can be counted on to work together, because of a built-in safety mechanism of American democracy. Welfare will not be abolished until the moral sanctions against illegitimacy have also gained great strength. There will not be enough votes until that mood is broad and deep.

It is only because of the sea change in the conventional wisdom about the deficiencies of single-parent families that proposals to end welfare are now being taken seriously. So far, that change has been couched in utilitarian terms. The next step, already well under way, is for language to change. Now, the elites are willing to say, "Having a baby if you are young and single is ill-advised." It seems to me that the truer way to put the issue is this: Bringing a new life into the world is one of the most profoundly important moral acts of a person's life. To bring a child into the world knowing that you are not intellectually, emotionally, or materially ready to care for that child is wrong.

When the elites are broadly willing to accept that formulation, and not before, welfare will be ended. And, at that stage, we can also be confident that the financial penalties of single parenthood—penalties that ending welfare would reimpose—are going to be reinforced by moral suasion.

Different parts of the country will reach this state of affairs sooner than others. In Utah, for example, with its low illegitimacy ratio plus the moral force of the Church of Latter Day Saints and that church's elaborate system of social welfare, one may be confident that if the entire federal welfare system disappeared tomorrow, the result would be overwhelmingly positive, with only the most minor new problems. But if the same legislation were to apply to Harlem, where more than 80 percent of children have been born out of wedlock for a decade and non-governmental social-welfare institutions are scattered and in disarray, one may be equally confident that the short-term result would be chaos on a massive scale.

Legislative Recommendations

Drawing these strands together, here are the characteristics of legislation that should be passed and might indeed have a reasonable chance of passing in the next several years.

• *The centerpiece of the legislation should be freedom for the states to experiment.* Congress knows that the welfare system it currently mandates for the entire country is a failure. The next thing for Congress to learn is that it does not have a one-size-fits-all answer to amend that failure. The solution is to permit the states to adopt a wide variety of plans. Thus, Congress should develop a simple formula whereby states can take the money that would otherwise flow into them in the form of AFDC payments, food stamps, and housing benefits (and as many other means-tested programs as possible) and use it for other ways of dealing with the needs of children currently supported by the welfare system. One example of a simple formula is to base the amount of the allocation on the budgets for those programs in the last year before the federal legislation is passed. States should also be permitted to end those programs altogether and forgo federal funds completely, though it is doubtful whether any state would choose to go that route.

Initially, most states would probably opt for modest reforms along the lines Congress is contemplating—more workfare, more job training, perhaps soft time limits. But a few brave states are likely to try something more ambitious. Probably one or two will adopt much more aggressive workfare or time limits than the ones in the Clinton plan. Perhaps a state somewhere will choose to adopt a version of the Kaus plan, funding public-service jobs in lieu of welfare benefits. My hope is that some state will also end welfare. If a state should consider doing so, below are some other guidelines that I would recommend.

• *Grandfather everyone now on the system, letting them retain their existing package of benefits under the existing rules.* The reasons for grandfathering are both ethical and pragmatic. For many women, welfare has turned out to be a Faustian bargain in which the government plays the role of the devil. Having made this bargain, many of the women on welfare are so mired in the habits of dependency and so bereft of job skills that it is unethical for the government now to demand that they pull themselves together. Pragmatically, grandfathering is probably a prerequisite for getting any such plan through a state legislature.

I should add that some grace period is also necessary

between the passage of the legislation and the time it takes effect. Nine months and one day is the symbolically correct period. Practically, a year seems about right: long enough to allow the word to spread, abrupt enough to preserve the shock value that is an essential part of changing behavior.

- *"Ending welfare" should mean at a minimum cutting off all payments which are contingent on or augmented by having a baby.* The core benefit to be ended altogether is AFDC. Medicaid benefits for the child should be left in place, because the existence of Medicaid has gutted the alternative ways in which medical care could be made reliably available to poor children (whereas there remain many alternative ways of providing children with food, shelter, and nurturing).

What about housing and food stamps? I doubt if it is possible to end them altogether. If a woman is poor enough to qualify for housing benefits and food stamps without a child, it seems unlikely that the courts would allow those benefits to be cut off because a child has been born. Instead, a state that adopts the "end-welfare" option should simply become neutral with regard to births out of wedlock. In principle, the best way for the state to become neutral is the approach advocated by free market economist Milton Friedman: Dismantle the entire social-welfare structure with its multiplicity of benefits and bureaucracies, replace it with a cash floor using the mechanism of the negative-income tax, and make that cash floor invariant regardless of the number of children. But I cannot imagine Congress giving states the option of converting all federal-subsidy programs into a negative-income tax (though it is certainly an intriguing idea). Some steps short of that need to be worked out.

One attractive possibility is to return to the original intention of the 1935 act that created welfare. AFDC would continue to be available for widows with young children and for divorced or abandoned women with young children, with a higher cash payment to compensate for the cuts in housing and food benefits. Unemployment benefits would also remain available for men and women alike, with or without children. I favor broadening and strengthening the unemployment-insurance system as part of this approach.

• *Limit the initial legislation to teenagers.* It is widely assumed that if welfare is ended, some other mechanisms will be required to replace it. Most of these options (I will describe some presently) involve extensive interventions *in loco parentis*. Limiting the initial legislation to teenagers has two merits. First, it is much better to let the government act *in loco parentis* for minors than for adults. Second, a political consensus already exists about single teenage girls having babies that has not yet consolidated about single adult women having babies.

Helping Single Mothers and Their Children

If a state ends welfare in the ways I have just described, a large behavioral impact may be expected—somewhere in the region of a 50 percent reduction in illegitimate births among whites (and probably among blacks as well) if the cross-state analyses are taken seriously.

Other effects are hard to predict. Some people assume that large numbers of pregnant women will move across the border to the next state, others predict a surge in abortions. The type and size of the effects will also depend on the nature of a state's caseload. The effects in a mostly rural plains or mountain state are likely to play out much differently than the effects in states with large cities. In any case, a substantial number of single women will continue to get pregnant. What happens to them and their children? These measures should be considered:

• *Actively support adoption at birth.* Today, the welfare system and its satellite social-work agencies typically discourage adoption. The pregnant single woman who wants to give up her child for adoption is more likely to be encouraged to keep the baby then to be praised. This is perverse. In America, the pool of mature, caring adoptive parents is deep, not just for perfect white babies but for children of all races and for children with physical and mental handicaps, *if*—the proviso is crucial—the child can be adopted at birth. Any comparison of what is known about child abuse and neglect, emotional development, or educational success suggests that the child of a never-married teenager has a better chance in an adoptive home.

If welfare has been ended, many more pregnant women will be looking at adoption, and the state can do much to help. Changes in laws can encourage a larger pool of adoptive parents by reinforcing the rights of the adoptive parents and by strictly limiting the rights of the biological parents. Adoption agencies can facilitate the adoption of black children by ending restrictions on transracial adoption.

• *Offer group living for pregnant women.* For a pregnant young woman from a functioning family and a functioning community, the best support network consists of friends and relatives. One of the chief reasons for ending welfare is to revitalize those networks. But one of the saddest aspects of today's burgeoning illegitimacy is that many pregnant young women have no friends and relatives who are competent to provide advice and nurturing during the pregnancy, let alone to help think through what will happen after the baby is born. This will continue to be true when welfare is ended.

States that end welfare should therefore look carefully at the experience of the homes for pregnant single women that dotted the country earlier in the century, most notably the Florence Crittendon homes. In a modern version of such a home, the young woman would receive the kind of prenatal care and diet—meaning, among other things, no drugs, alcohol, or tobacco—that would help children of unwed mothers get off to a better physiological start. Group homes of this sort can also be excellent places to help young women come to grips with their problems and prepare for their futures.

• *Offer group living for teenage single mothers.* Another intriguing suggestion is to extend the Florence Crittendon concept to the period after birth. The mother who keeps her baby is no longer given welfare services, but she is given the option to live in a group home. She and her child receive food and shelter; the mother receives training in parenting and job skills; and the child is in an environment where at least some of the adults understand the needs of infants and small children.

• *Maintain a clear, bright line short of coercion.* Adoption services or group homes must be purely optional; no young woman should be required to use these services. This bears on a broader point. Having a baby you are not prepared to care for is wrong, but this does not mean that the state has the right to prevent you from doing it—a nice distinction between immoral acts and the state's power to regulate them that could easily be ignored once the Left decides that illegitimacy is a bad thing. An idea gaining favor—requiring welfare recipients to use Norplant—illustrates the danger. From a legal standpoint, I find nothing objectionable about the idea. Welfare is not a right but largesse, and the state may legitimately place conditions upon dispensing largesse. But once the government requires any use of birth control, a barrier has been broken that has frightening possibilities.

For the same reason, the government must be passive regarding the encouragement of abortion. If enough people think that low-income women should have easier access to abortions, let the subsidies come from the philanthropies that private citizens choose to support. The process of ending welfare must unambiguously represent a withdrawal of the state from personal decisions, not new intrusions.

• *Enforce the existing laws on child neglect.* One of the most common questions about ending welfare is, "What happens to the woman who keeps her baby anyway?" The answer is that some women will indeed choose to keep their babies. As I have already suggested, the self-selection process imposed by the end of welfare also means that such women are likely to be those who have the greatest commitment to their children. They are likely to be the ones who have done the best job of lining up support from relatives and friends, or the ones who have well-paying jobs.

But the main point is that single women who keep their

babies will be in exactly the same situation as every other parent who takes a baby home from the hospital: that child is now the parent's responsibility. There is no need to keep a special watch on how a single mother does; rather, she falls under the same laws regarding child neglect and abuse as everyone else, to be enforced in the same way.

And that finally, should be the overriding theme of what we do about welfare: treating the human drama of "having a child" as the deeply solemn, responsibility-laden act that it is, and treating all parents the same in their obligation to be good parents. The government does not have the right to prescribe how people shall live or to prevent women from having babies. It should not have the right even to encourage certain women to have babies through the granting of favors. But for sixty years the government has been granting those favors, and thereby intervening in a process that human communities know how to regulate much better than governments do. Welfare for single mothers has been destructive beyond measure, and it should be stopped forthwith.

Notes:

[1]"Welfare and the Family: The American Experience," *Journal of Labor Economics* (January 1993), and "Does Welfare Bring More Babies?" *Public Interest* (Spring 1994).

[2]The NLSY is a very large (originally 12,686 persons) nationally representative sample of American youths who were aged 14 to 22 in 1979, when the study began, and who have been followed ever since.

Marvin Olasky

The New Welfare Debate: How to Practice Effective Compassion

For too long the welfare debate has been the "same old same old." Liberals have emphasized distribution of bread and assumed the poor could live on that alone. Conservatives have complained about the mold on the bread and pointed out the waylaying of funds by "welfare queens" and the empire-building of "poverty pimps."

It is time now, however, to talk not about reforming the welfare system—which often means scraping off a bit of mold—but about replacing it with a revolutionary, centrist system based on private and religious charity. Such a system was effective in the nineteenth century and will be even more effective in the twenty-first century, with the decentralization that new technology makes possible, if we make the right changes in personal goals and public policy.

Why is welfare replacement necessary? Because in America we now face not just concern about poor individuals falling between the cracks, but the crunch of sidewalks disintegrating. An explosive growth in the number of children born out of wedlock—in 1995, one of every three of our fellow citizens is beginning life hindered by the absence of a father—is one indication of rapid decline.

Why is welfare replacement politically possible? Because there is broad understanding that the system hurts the very

61

people it was designed to help, and that the trillions of dollars spent in the name of compassion over the past three decades have largely been wasted. Conservatives who want an opportunity to recover past wisdom and apply it to future practice should thank liberals for providing a wrecked ship. And liberals should support welfare replacement because, given the mood of the country, the alternative to replacement is not an expanded welfare state, but an extinct one.

Why is welfare replacement morally right? Because, when we look at the present system, we are dealing with not just the dispersal of dollars but the destruction of lives. When William Tecumseh Sherman's army marched through Georgia in 1864, about 25,000 blacks followed his infantry columns, until Sherman and his soldiers decided to rid themselves of the followers by hurrying across an unfordable stream and then taking up the pontoon bridge, leaving the ex-slaves stranded on the opposite bank. Many tried to swim across but died in the icy water. Similarly today, many of the stranded poor will soon be abandoned by a country that has seen welfare failure and is lapsing into a skeptical and even cynical "compassion syndrome"—unless we find a way to renew the American dream of compassion.

The destruction of life through the current welfare system is not often so dramatic as that which occurred in 1864, but the death of dreams is evident every day. During the past three decades, we have seen lives destroyed and dreams die among poor individuals who have gradually become used to dependency. Those who stressed independence used to be called the "worthy poor"; now, a person who will not work is also worthy, and mass pauperism is accepted. Now, those who are willing to put off immediate gratification and to sacrifice leisure time in order to remain independent are called chumps rather than champs.

We have also seen dreams die among some social workers who had been in the forefront of change. Their common lament is, "All we have time to do is move paper." Those who really care do not last long, and one who resigned cried out, "I had a calling; it was that simple. I wanted to help." Some social workers take satisfaction in meeting demands, but others who want to change lives become despondent in their role of enabling destructive behavior.

We have seen dreams die as "compassion fatigue" deepens. Personal involvement is down, cynicism is up. Many of us would like to be generous at the subway entrance or the street corner, but we know that most homeless recipients will use any available funds for drugs or alcohol. We end up walking by, avoiding eye contact—and a subtle hardening occurs once more. Many of us would like to contribute more of our money and time to the poor, but we are weighed down by heavy tax burdens. We end up just saying "no" to personal involvement, and a sapping of citizenship occurs once more. We have seen dreams die among children who will never know their fathers. Government welfare programs have contributed to the removal of fathers, and nothing can replace them.

Some would say that for the poor and the fatherless the death of dreams is inevitable, but that is not so. England in the nineteenth century recovered from its downward spiral which began in the eighteenth century. And the United States in the twenty-first century can recover from our recent problems, since we know a great deal from our own experience about how to fight poverty. We had successful anti-poverty programs a century ago—successful because they embodied personal, material, and spiritual involvement and challenge.

This vital story has generally been ignored by liberal historians, but the documented history goes like this: During the nineteenth century, a successful war on poverty was waged by tens of thousands of local, private charitable agencies and religious groups around the country. The platoons of the greatest charity army in American history often were small. They were made up of volunteers led by poorly paid but deeply dedicated professional managers. And they were highly effective.

Thousands of eyewitness accounts and journalistic assessments show that poverty fighters of the nineteenth century did not abolish poverty, but they enabled millions of people to escape it. They saw springs of fresh water flowing among the poor, not just blocks of ice sitting in a perpetual winter of multi-generational welfare dependency. And the optimism prevalent then contrasts sharply with the demoralization among the poor and the cynicism among the better-off that is so common now.

What was their secret? It was not neglect. It was their understanding of the literal and biblical meaning of compassion, which comes from two Latin words—*com*, which means "with," and *pati*, which means "to suffer." The word points to personal involvement with the needy, suffering with them, not just giving to them. "Suffering with" means adopting hard-to-place babies, providing shelter to women undergoing crisis pregnancies, becoming a big brother to a fatherless child, working one-on-one with a young single mother. It is not easy—but it works.

Our predecessors did not have it easy—but they persevered. Theirs were not "the good old days." Work days were long and affluence was rare, and homes on the average were much smaller than ours. There were severe drug and alcohol problems and many more early deaths from disease. We are more spread out now, but our travel time is not any greater. Overall, most of the problems paralleled our own; the big difference lies in the rates of increase in illegitimacy and divorce. Most of the opportunities and reasons to help also were similar; a big difference in this regard is that our tax burden is much larger, and many Americans justifiably feel that they are already paying for others to take care of the needy.

In the nineteenth century, volunteers opened their own homes to deserted women and orphaned children. They offered employment to nomadic men who had abandoned hope and most human contact. Most significantly, our predecessors made moral demands on recipients of aid. They saw family, work, freedom, and faith as central to our being, not as lifestyle options. The volunteers gave of their own lives not just so that others might survive, but that they might thrive.

Seven Basic Principles of Effective Compassion

Our predecessors also developed seven basic principles of compassion:

Affiliation

A century ago, when individuals applied for material assistance, charity volunteers tried first to "restore family ties that have been sundered" and "reabsorb in social life those who for some reason have snapped the threads that bound them to other members of the community." Instead of immediately offering help, charities asked, "Who is bound to help in this case?" In 1897, Mary Richmond of the Baltimore Charity Organizing Society summed up the wisdom of a century: "Relief given without reference to friends and neighbors is accompanied by moral loss. Poor neighborhoods are doomed to grow poorer whenever the natural ties of neighborliness are weakened by well-meant but unintelligent interference."

Today, before developing a foundation project or contributing to a private charity, we should ask, "Does it work through families, neighbors, and religious or community organizations, or does it supersede them?" For example, studies show that many homeless alcoholics have families, but they do not want to be with them. When homeless shelters provide food, clothing, and housing without asking hard questions, aren't they subsidizing disaffiliation and enabling addiction? Instead of giving aid directly to homeless men, why not work on reuniting them with brothers, sisters, parents, wives, or children?

We should ask as well whether other programs help or hurt. It is good to help an unmarried teenager mother, but much of such aid now offers a mirage of independence. A better plan is to reunite her whenever possible with those on whom she actually depends, whether she admits it or not: her parents and the child's father. It is good to give Christmas presents to poor children, but when the sweet-minded "helper" shows up with a shiny new fire truck that outshines the second-hand items a poor single mom put together, the damage is done. A better plan is to bulwark the beleaguered mom by enabling her to provide a better present.

Bonding

When applicants for help a century ago were truly alone, volunteers worked one-to-one to become, in essence, new family members. Charity volunteers a century ago usually were not assigned to massive food-dispensing tasks, but were given the narrow but deep responsibility of making a difference in one life over several years. Kindness and firmness were both essential. In 1898, the magazine *American Hebrew* told of how one man was sunk into dependency but a volunteer "with great patience convinced him that he must earn his living." Soon he did, and he regained the respect of his family and community. Similarly, a woman had become demoralized, but "for months she was worked with, now through kindness, again through discipline, until finally she began to show a desire to help herself."

Today, when an unmarried pregnant teenager is dumped by her boyfriend and abandoned by angry parents who refuse to be reconciled, she needs a haven, a room in a home with a volunteer family. When a single mom at the end of her rope cannot take care of a toddler, he should be placed quickly for adoption where a new and permanent bonding can take place, rather than rotated through a succession of foster homes.

Categorization

Charities a century ago realized that two persons in exactly the same material circumstances but with different values need different treatment: One might benefit most from some material help and a pat on the back, the other might need spiritual challenge and a push. Those who were orphaned, elderly, or disabled received aid; jobless adults who were "able and willing to work" received help in job-finding; those who preferred "to live on alms" and those of "confirmed intemperance" were not entitled to material assistance.

"Work tests" helped both in sorting and in providing relief with dignity. When an able-bodied man came to a homeless shelter, he often was asked to chop wood for two hours or whitewash a building; in that way he could provide part of his own support and also help those unable to perform these chores. A needy woman generally was given a seat in the "sewing room" (often near a child care room) and asked to work on garments that would be donated to the helpless poor or sent through the Red Cross to families suffering from the effects of hurricanes, floods, or other natural disasters. The work test, along with teaching good habits and keeping away those who did not really need help, also enabled charities to teach the lesson that those who were being helped could help others.

Today, we need to stop talking about "the poor" in abstraction and start distinguishing once again between those who truly yearn for help and those who just want an enabler. Programs have the chance to succeed only when categories are established and firmly maintained. Work tests can help: Why shouldn't some homeless men clean up streets and parks and remove graffiti? Now, as thousands of crack babies (born addicted to cocaine and often deserted by mothers who care only for the next high) languish in hospitals and shelters under bright lights and with almost no human contact, why shouldn't homeless women (those who are healthy and gentle) be assigned to hold a baby for an hour in exchange for food and shelter?

Discernment

"Intelligent giving and intelligent withholding are alike true charity," the New Orleans Charity Organization Society declared in 1899. It added, "If drink has made a man poor, money will feed not him, but his drunkenness." Poverty-fighters a century ago trained volunteers to leave behind "a conventional attitude toward the poor, seeing them through the comfortable haze of our own intentions." Barriers against fraud were important not only to prevent waste but to preserve morale among those who *were* working hard to remain independent: "Nothing," declared the Society, "is more demoralizing to the struggling poor than successes of the indolent."

Bad charity also created uncertainty among givers as to how their contributions would be used and thus led to less giving over the long term. It was important to "reform those mild, well-meaning, tender-hearted, sweet-voiced criminals who insist upon indulging in indiscriminate charity." Compassion was greatest when givers could "work with safety, confidence, and liberty." Today, lack of discernment in helping poor individuals is rapidly producing an anti-compassion backlash, as the better-off, unable to distinguish between the truly needy and the "grubby-grabby," give to neither.

Employment

Nineteenth century New York charity leader Josephine Lowell wrote that "the problem before those who would be charitable, is not how to deal with a given number of the poor; it is how to help those who are poor, without adding to their numbers and constantly increasing the evils they seek to cure." If people were paid for not working, the number of non-workers would increase, and children would grow up without seeing work as a natural and essential part of life. Individuals had to accept responsibility: Governmental programs operating without the discipline of the marketplace were inherently flawed, because their payout came "from what is regarded as a practically inexhaustible source, and people who once receive it are likely to regard it as a right, as a permanent pension, implying no obligation on their part."

In the twentieth century and beyond, programs that stress employment, sometimes in creative ways, need new emphasis.

For example, instead of temporary housing, more of the able-bodied might receive the opportunity to work for a permanent home through "sweat equity" arrangements in which labor constitutes most of the down payment. Some who start in rigorous programs of this sort drop out with complaints that too much sweat is required, but one person who stayed in such a program said at the end, "We are poor, but we have something that is ours. When you use your own blood, sweat, and tears, it's part of your soul. You stand and say, 'I did it.'"

Freedom

Charity workers a century ago did not press for governmental programs, but instead showed poor people how to move up while resisting enslavement to governmental masters. Job freedom was the opportunity to drive a wagon without paying bribes, to cut hair without having to go to barber college, and to get a foot on the lowest rung of the ladder, even if wages there were low. Freedom was the opportunity for a family to escape dire poverty by having a father work long hours and a mother sew garments at home. Life was hard, but static, multigenerational poverty of the kind we now have was rare; those who persevered could star in a motion picture of upward mobility.

Today, in our desire to make the bottom rung of the economic ladder higher, we have cut off the lowest rungs and left many on the ground. Those who are pounding the pavements looking for work and those who have fallen between the cracks are hindered by what is supposed to help them. Mother Teresa's plan to open a homeless shelter in New York was stopped by a building code that required an elevator; nuns in her order said that they would carry upstairs anyone who could not walk, but the city stuck to its guns and the shelter never opened. In Texas and New Mexico, a Bible-based anti-drug program run by Victory Fellowship has a 60 percent success rate in beating addiction, yet the Commission on Drug and

Alcohol Abuse has instructed the program to stop calling itself one of "drug rehabilitation" because it does not conform to bureaucratic standards.

God

"True philanthropy must take into account spiritual as well as physical needs," poverty-fighters a century ago noted, and both Christians and Jews did. Bible-believing Christians worshipped a God who came to earth and showed in life and death the literal meaning of compassion—*suffering with.* Jewish teaching stressed the pursuit of righteousness through the doing of good deeds. Groups such as the Industrial Christian Alliance noted that they used "religious methods"—reminding the poor that God made them and had high expectations for them—to "restore the fallen and helpless to self-respect and self-support."

Today, challenge that goes beyond the material is still essential to poverty-fighting. In Washington, D.C., multimillion-dollar programs have failed, but, a mile from the U.S. Capitol, success stories are developing: Spiritually-based programs such as Clean and Sober Streets, where ex-alcoholics and ex-addicts help those still in captivity; the Gospel Mission, which fights homelessness by offering true hope; and the Capitol Hill Crisis Pregnancy Center, where teenage moms and their children, born and unborn, are cared for, are all saving lives. In Dallas, Texas, a half-mile from the Dallas Housing Authority's failed projects, a neighborhood group called Voice of Hope invites teenagers to learn about God through Bible studies and to work at remodeling deteriorated homes in their neighborhood. During the past decade, crime rates among the boys involved with Voice of Hope and pregnancy rates among the girls have been dramatically lower than those in the surrounding community.

Changing Our Methods of Fighting Poverty

What this understanding adds up to is the sense that we need
to change our methods of fighting poverty, but we need to be
clear about the reasons for change. Government welfare programs should be replaced not because they are too expensive—although, clearly, much money is wasted—but because
they are inevitably too stingy in providing what is truly important: treating people as human beings made in God's image,
not as animals to be fed and caged.

Private charities can do a better job than government, but
only if they practice the principles of effective compassion. *Giving*, by itself, we need to remember, is morally neutral. We
need to give *rightly*, so as not to impede the development of values that enable people to get out of poverty and stay out. Only
when the seven principles of effective compassion noted above
are widely understood and practiced, can anti-poverty work
succeed. In 1995, as in 1895, the best programs offer challenge, not just enabling, and they deal with spiritual questions
as well as material needs. In 1995, as in 1895, there is no effective substitute for the hard process of one person helping
another. And the century-old question—Does any given
"scheme of help...make great demands on men to give themselves to their brethren?"—is still the right one to ask.

David Green

Welfare Before the Welfare State: The British Experience

There are three main reasons for studying welfare before the welfare state. First, we need to discover better ways of providing welfare services today. In many respects, welfare before the welfare state was better. Second, the West is suffering from a measure of moral breakdown whose roots lie at least partly in the replacement of voluntary associations by the state. Voluntary associations not only provide services, they also serve a vital educational and character-building role indispensable to liberty. Third, we need to improve our understanding of how best to distribute responsibility throughout the community, as a bulwark against over-mighty government. The welfare state has become a rationale for the concentration of political power and the direction of people's lives by the authorities.

Organized private welfare falls into two categories: philanthropy and mutual aid.

Philanthropy

First, I will briefly describe the scope of philanthropy in Britain, and second, something of its spirit as compared with the welfare state.

The leading historians of philanthropy have not been able

73

to gauge its full extent, since it was spontaneous and dispersed. A recent study by Geoffrey Finlayson quotes a contemporary estimate which put the annual expenditure of private charities in London in 1870 at between £5.5 million and £7 million, when London contained about ten percent of the population.[1] If total charitable giving in England and Wales is put at £55 million, it dwarfs the total expenditure on poor relief in England and Wales of £8 million in 1871.

Tithing was common practice. A survey of forty-two middle-class families in the 1890s showed that on average they spent 10.7 percent of their income on charity, more than on rent, clothing, servants' wages or anything else except food.[2]

Schools

State schooling was introduced in Britain in 1879, but before that date the Newcastle Commission had reported in 1861 that "almost everyone receives some amount of schooling at some period or another." The growth of private schooling between 1818 and 1858 had been rapid, far exceeding the growth in the population. In 1818, the number of day pupils was 675,000; in 1833, 1.3 million; 1851, 2.1 million; and 1858, 2.5 million. The average duration of schooling had also increased. In 1858, the Newcastle Commission put it at nearly six years.[3]

Charity schools had mostly been founded during the eighteenth century to teach poor children the alphabet and the principles of religion. They were followed in the 1780s by the Sunday-school movement, which stressed moral teaching as well as literacy and numeracy and the "schools of industry," which taught children to be industrious.

Hospitals

Voluntary hospitals were established in London and most of the large towns during the eighteenth century. Towards the end of that century, the dispensary movement developed to supply medicines and organize district and home visiting in place of hospital attendance. Later, these free dispensaries came under criticism for creating dependency, and provident dispensaries were founded to allow patients to pay a low fixed subscription, with the balance from charity. It was considered more dignified than paying nothing.

When hospitals were nationalized in Britain in 1948, the voluntary hospitals were providing the backbone of the acute hospital service. Nearly 60 percent of patients requiring acute care were admitted to voluntary hospitals in 1936.[4] They also provided the overwhelming majority of teaching hospitals. The best pre-nationalization source of information is a report by Political and Economic Planning (PEP), "The British Health Services," published in 1937. It was written by socialists who wanted a state hospital service, but they found it necessary to report that in 1935, while unemployment was still high, the voluntary hospitals had an annual surplus income of over £1 million. The authors of the PEP report can only give grudging praise, conceding that "despite the depression," the majority of voluntary hospitals have "temporarily" overcome their financial difficulties.[5]

Voluntary hospitals originally provided free care, but concern grew that it was degrading to rely on charity and movements evolved to allow people to pay. Hospital contributory schemes (a kind of pre-paid insurance) developed rapidly during the second half of the nineteenth century to allow people in lower income groups to make regular contributions entitling them, without further inquiry into their means, to receive free hospital treatment for themselves and their dependents. By 1936 at least 10 million persons were covered.

This record of the voluntary hospitals has a double significance. They had not only been providing an improving service for decades by the time they were nationalized but also had been providing a focal point for people of goodwill in the locality. Individuals could help as hospital visitors, or as fund raisers if that was where their talent lay, or in providing "extras" like books for patients to read or in running a voluntary canteen. The hospitals were outlets for all those human decencies, great and small, which make life worthwhile. Under nationalization, the tendency was for all services to be provided by paid staff, guided less by altruism and more by their trade union rule book.

Philanthropy and the Poor

Now let me concentrate on three questions: first, how the problem of poverty was perceived; second, how the beneficiaries of charity were seen, and especially whether they were classified into the "deserving" and "undeserving," and third, what were the relative responsibilities of the individual, the community and the state?

From "the poor" to "poverty" to "the victim"

During the eighteenth century and until the end of the nineteenth century, philanthropists devoted themselves to "the poor." Sir Frederick Eden's classic study, *The State of the Poor*, published in 1796, focused on "the poor," a term that implied that the poor were always with us. It led to the dole charities which parceled out aid in cash or kind.

By the middle of the century, a new view was beginning to dominate: that the problem was one of "poverty," which could be eradicated. The Charity Organization Society (COS) had been founded in 1869 to campaign against the "dole charities," which gave only cash support to the poor. The Society felt that this practice had a demoralizing effect and pressed for a new approach that sought to restore independence and bring out the best in people rather than to reinforce their dependence on others. It soon had branches or offshoots in most of the larger towns in Great Britain, the Colonies, and the United States.

Later in the nineteenth century, two additional views developed among those who saw poverty as eradicable. One group thought it was the duty of the state, the other the community. C. S. Loch, the secretary of the Charity Organization Society, argued that to speak of poverty in the manner of Booth (whose *Life and Labor of the People in London* was published between 1891 and 1903) and Rowntree (who studied poverty in York in 1899) was to see the problem—mistakenly—as one of money alone and the public policy issue as how best to get additional money to some people. But money was not the real problem, according to Loch. He believed it was one of "social habit." People of similar means, he said, do not live in the same way, and if some were poor the real challenge was to discover what it was in their background or lifestyle that could be changed in order to restore their independence.[6] Indiscriminate relief, he said, "attracts the applicant by an appeal to his weakness, and it requires of him no effort." He preferred to appeal to the strength of the applicant and to require an effort on his part.[7]

During the twentieth century, however, poverty came to be seen more and more as the responsibility of the state. By the 1960s, these arguments had been forgotten and the demoralizing of the less fortunate had gone further still. Relative poverty was presented as a progressive doctrine, but in reality it has more in common with the old doctrine of "the poor." It defines poverty so that some percentage of the population will always be poor. A common method is to treat those with less than 50 percent of the average (or median) wage as poor, thus entrenching dependency. No less important, its protagonists have gotten away with presenting anyone who criticizes their view as inhumane. It is common to accuse anyone who draws attention to personal responsibility of "blaming the victim." All human conduct, in this view is the result of outside forces: "the system." The public policy conclusion is that political power should be used to modify the "outside forces." (The counter emphasis, represented today by writers like Charles Murray, is on finding ways for everyone to escape poverty by becoming as independent as possible.)

The Deserving and Undeserving

The Charity Organization Society is often presented as rather harsh and too quick to distinguish between the deserving and the undeserving poor. But that was not the dominant view. C.S. Loch put it another way. The problem, he said:

> is not whether the person is "deserving" or "undeserving," but whether, granted the facts, the distress can be stayed and self-support attained. If the help can be given privately from within the circle of the family, so much the better. Sometimes it may be best to advise, but not to interfere. In some cases but little help may be necessary; in others again the friendly relation between applicant and friend may last for months and even years.[8]

The ideal to aim for was mutual respect between giver and taker: no presumption of superiority by the giver, and no doffing of caps by the receiver. This spirit is captured by an incident in Dickens' *Hard Times* when Stephen Blackpool, an honest and hard-working power-loom weaver in Josiah Bounderby's factory, is unfairly sacked. His plight is desperate, for he has no money and no chance of other work in the locality without a reference from Bounderby. He faces a long and arduous journey by foot in search of employment. Bounderby's wife, who believes her husband was unjust, offers Stephen a bank note to see him through the hard times ahead. He takes only £2, a much smaller sum than she offered because, he says, he knows he can pay that much back.[9] In other words, despite his dire predicament, he will not allow the relationship to be one-sided and will accept only a loan. Mutual respect between giver and receiver was maintained.

The giving of help is undoubtedly difficult to accomplish in the right spirit, and during the last century great effort was expended to discover and encourage the right approach. The charities of that time provided their employees and volunteers with guidelines or manuals to instill mutual respect. Some of these guidelines have been described in an excellent study of philanthropy by F.K. Prochaska. Mutual respect was the essence:

> Remember, it is a "privilege" not a "right" to enter the poor man's cottage. Be sympathetic, not patronizing. Be a friend, not a relieving lady. Avoid giving money. Do not promote a spirit of dependence. Distinguish cases of real misery from those of fictitious distress. Avoid favoritism. Be an expert on domestic management. Quote the Scriptures. Avoid religious controversy. Encourage school attendance. Avoid politics. "Show that almsgiving is not merely the duty of the rich, but also the privilege of the poor." Be regular in your visits.[10]

The Individual, the Community and the State

Lord Beveridge cites William Akroyd speaking at a gathering of poor law guardians in 1841: "Before it is just to say that a man ought to be an independent laborer, the country ought to be in such a state that a laborer by honest industry can become independent."[11] The dominant view during the nineteenth century was not that all problems were individual, but rather that a combination of effort by the individual, the community and the state was required. But when observers emphasized that there must be a common effort, they did not only mean that the government must do something. There was a strong communal sense distinct from the state.

The COS urged its visitors to give charity not as "from strangers to strangers" but as a transaction between people personally known to each other. Only in such a personal relationship would the rich appreciate "the responsibility attaching to wealth and leisure" and the poor have "the comfortable assurance that if the day of exceptional adversity should come, they will not be left to encounter it without a friend."[12]

They were not blind to the role of the state. Charities sought social reform. According to Loch, the duty of charity was to seek both to intensify the sense of membership of society and also to improve social conditions through legal reform.[13]

Shaftesbury, for example, had pushed through the factory acts, while others urged prison reform, child protection laws, housing reform, and much more.

The primary responsibility for welfare in a free society lay with the individual and his family, but no one should be left to cope alone. The community, in the form of voluntary associations, should always be there to help and the state should be in the background, ready to help, but within proper limits. So in essence responsibility was shared between the state, the community and the individual. There was a state minimum, resort to which was considered to be "letting the side down." The community took responsibility for helping people in order to avoid the taint of pauperism. Thus, there was the certainty of minimum help, combined with the likelihood of fuller personal assistance given voluntarily.

Mutual Aid

The scale of charity was enormous, but it affected far fewer people than mutual aid. Three quarters of those covered by the 1911 National Insurance Act were already members of friendly societies: 9.5 million out of 12 million. Future Prime Minister Lloyd George, when introducing the bill, argued that it was his intention to make available to everyone the benefits already being provided for themselves by the great majority. In 1910, the last full year before the 1911 Act, there were 6.6 million members of registered friendly societies, quite apart from those in unregistered societies. The rate of growth of the friendly societies over the preceding thirty years had been rapid and was accelerating. In 1877, registered membership had been 2.8 million. Ten years later, it was 3.6 million, increasing at an average of 90,000 a year. In 1897, membership had reached 4.8 million, having increased an average by 120,000 a year. And by 1910, the figure had reached 6.6 million, having increased at an annual average rate since 1897 of

140,000.[14] Friendly society membership far exceeded that of the other characteristic organizations of the working classes, the trade unions and the cooperative societies. In 1910 there were 6.6 million registered members of friendly societies, 2.5 million members of registered trade unions, and 2.5 million members of cooperative societies.[15]

Ethos

The societies sharply contrasted themselves with charities. Charity was one set of people helping another set; mutual aid was putting money aside in a common fund and helping each other when the need arose. As one leading society put it, the benefits were rights:

> For certain benefits in sickness...[we] subscribe to one fund. That fund is our Bank; and to draw therefrom is the independent and manly right of every Member, whenever the contingency for which the funds are subscribed may arise, as freely as if the fund was in the hand of their own banker, and they had but to issue a check for the amount. These are not BENEVOLENCES—they are rights.

This language of rights was later purloined by the welfare state, but by then it meant something very different.

Character Building

The societies were not just benefit societies. They sought to foster the values that make freedom possible. New members underwent an initiation ceremony which was to be only their first taste of the ritual which would form a regular part of lodge life. The Manchester Unity had a series of four degrees which were progressively awarded to members as they came to play a fuller part in the running of the lodge. The degrees took the form of ceremonies lasting, perhaps, fifteen minutes. On each occasion the member received a lecture from the chairman, and was given a secret grip, sign and password. Other societies explained their ideals to members in a series of lectures.

These values included solidarity: a shared commitment to maintain the institutions fundamental to liberty; "doing your bit." They emphasized fraternity, and they provided training in skills necessary for democracy: Offices were shared to give members status and the opportunity to test their talents.

The Ancient Order of Foresters did not confine its advice, given during its course of seven lectures, to the conduct of society business. It urged new members as follows:

> In your domestic relationships we look to find you, if a husband, affectionate and trustful; if a father, regardful of the moral and material well-being of your children and dependents; as a son, dutiful and exemplary, and as a friend, steadfast and true.

In the Grand United Order of Oddfellows, the new member was encouraged to make the moment of joining not only a time of self-criticism, but also an occasion for the very remolding of his character:

> It is desired that you should make the event of your Initiation a time for strict self-examination; and if you should find anything in your past life to amend, I solemnly charge you to set about that duty without delay,—let no immoral practice, idle action, or low and vulgar pursuit, be retained by you.

The Spirit of Independence

In 1882, the leader of the AOF argued against compulsory state pensions and spoke with pride of how fewer and fewer people were dependent on the state. J.L. Stead, the permanent secretary of the Foresters, expressed his pride in the fact that his society had low-paid members: "We have got some of the humblest men in the country in our society, and we are just as proud of them as of the others."[16]

Receipt of Poor Relief, 1849–1908

Year	Number	Percent
1849	1,088,659	6.3
1852	915,675	5.1
1862	917,142	4.6
1872	977,200	4.3
1882	788,289	3.1
1892	744,757	2.6

Source: Royal Commission on the Poor Laws, 1909.

The Services

The common element to all the services was independence. Societies provided all the services which enabled people to be self-supporting:

1. Earnings when the breadwinner was ill or injured.
2. Support for the widow and orphans when the breadwinner died.
3. Support in old age. The ethos, however, was different. The usual attitude was to keep working as long as possible with the fall-back of sick pay.
4. Traveling in search of work (including internationally). (The correct handshake and password proved more effective than today's social security numbers in discouraging fraud.)
5. Medical care when ill. Usually doctors were paid a capitation fee in return for free care. But the societies also organized medical institutes where service was provided by salaried medical officers.

Conclusions

The argument is not that the friendly societies and charities always hit upon better ways of doing things. Many also made mistakes, but this, too, was valuable. One of the most important lessons of history is that there is no perfection in human affairs. The human condition is to struggle for improvement, and once we have hit upon successful formulae to struggle again to maintain them. We never know what the future holds, and for this reason we should make arrangements which speed up the process by which we learn from experience. Private welfare allowed trial and error. Beveridge remarked how often some of the finest organizations had begun as meetings of a dozen people in a back room somewhere. Public sector monopoly acts on the exactly contrary principle. It assumes there is one obvious right answer and that the state can achieve the desired outcome most effectively. The history of welfare teaches us the folly of any such assumption.

For instance, during the second half of the nineteenth century there was a vigorous debate between the "dole charities" that confined themselves to giving out cash and the friendly-visiting charities that emphasized the importance of personal support and criticized donors who were content to give cash and to disregard character. People were urged to give practical help, or to support charities which offered personal support. This argument was played out during the nineteenth century between protagonists in language strikingly reminiscent of today's worries about dependency.

The argument is not that in a competitive system we always arrive at the right answer. It is that by allowing many people to back their judgment at their own risk, we arrive sooner at the right answers. We learn from the successes and failures of others. When government assumed responsibility for the poor, it adopted the dole charity model. It has proved far more difficult to correct that error than it did during the nineteenth century when critics did not have to fight a political campaign but could more readily put their ideas to the test of experience. As in so many things, the undue concentration of power is the enemy of welfare.

There is also a more general reason for studying the history of welfare. We urgently need to refresh our understanding of the ideal of a free society. Until the collapse of the Berlin Wall in 1989, the twentieth century was dominated by the battle between two economic systems: a planned economy and a market economy. The ideal of freedom is not only a free economy—allowing the free play of self-interest, the fluctuation of supply and demand, competition, and favoring private over state owned property. It is also about encouraging and harnessing the best in people, including the full gamut of human motivations and ideals. It is about character, virtue, intelligence, measuring up to challenges, facing difficulties. In the fight against communism the moral dimension was sometimes forgotten in the heat of battle. This omission was yet another of the costs of communism, which defined the battle in purely economic terms.

Now that communism is out of the way we need to develop the ideal of liberty further. It should embrace a free economy, the freedom to make money, but also the duties that go with success.

It does not follow that the duty to care for the less fortunate should be required by law. On the contrary, such duties are best encouraged by public opinion. And defenders of a free society should acknowledge that a free economy on its own lacks moral credentials without a corresponding philosophy to care for the less fortunate.

There needs to be a place for everyone, including those who are not very confident about their ability to adopt, adjust and hold down "a portfolio of jobs." But there are traps. In the postcommunist era, socialism is reformulating its message in less economic terms. First, it aims its appeal at those who lack confidence in their ability to cope. If it only offered assurance of help—a second chance, a safety net, a helping hand—there would be no difficulty. But socialism is not satisfied to offer a helping hand. It is a rationale for the concentration of power. It sees people as victims of circumstance, and it aspires to use political power to alter those circumstances. It sees people, not as personally responsible, but as role players in permanent need of paternalistic guidance.

Second, socialism appeals to the human need for a sense of community or belonging. Again, it taps into a worthy sentiment. But once more, it demands a high price. Its adherents do not stop at intensifying our sense of belonging. Socialists want to decide in the political process what is in the common good and to direct human affairs by force. Thus, the new socialism is about tapping worthy sentiments—the desire to help, the desire to contribute to the common good, to belong—and politicizing them. It sees the state as the only agent of change.

Experience of welfare before the welfare state teaches us how to get the balance right. Yes a helping hand, yes a sense of community. But not political direction of individual lives or pretending that the political system *is* the community. There can be, and was, a "public but not political" domain. There was and could be again, "community without politics."

Notes:

[1] G. Finlayson, *Citizen, State, and Social Welfare in Britain 1830–1990* (Oxford: Clarendon Press, 1994), 63; "Report of the Royal Commission on the Poor Laws (London: HMSO, 1909), 26.

[2] F.K. Prochaska, *Women and Philanthropy in Nineteenth-Century England* (Oxford: Clarendon Press, 1980), 21.

[3] E.G. West, "Education Without the State," *Economic Affairs*, Vol. 14, No. 5 (1994), 13.

[4] "The British Health Services" (London: Political and Economic Planning, 1937), 257.

[5] Ibid., 232.

[6] C.S. Loch, *Charity and Social Life* (London: Macmillan, 1910), 387.

[7] Ibid., 401

[8] Ibid., 400

[9]C. Dickens, *Hard Times* (London: Pan Books, 1977), 165–66.

[10]Prochaska, F.K., 113–14.

[11]W. Beveridge, *Voluntary Action* (London: George Allen & Unwin, 1948), 7.

[12]Himmelfarb, 367.

[13]Loch, 367.

[14]D.G. Green, *Working Class Patients and the Medical Establishment* (London: Gover/Temple Smith, 1985), 179.

[15]Beveridge, 92, 328 (trade union membership is for 1912; see below p. 42 for fuller analysis of friendly society membership); P. Johnson, *Saving and Spending: The Working Class Economy in Britain 1870–1939* (Oxford: Clarendon Press, 1985), 7607.

[16]Ibid., *Appendix VII, 77543–44.*

Dwight R. Lee

Poverty, Politics, and Personal Responsibility

The Speaker of the House Newt Gingrich recently pointed out that (and I am paraphrasing just a bit here) there is no escalator built by redistribution on which you can sit while government carries you up. It does not exist. It is not possible. Gingrich is right. Until poor people are willing to assume responsibility for the consequences of their actions, there is nothing anyone, or any program, can do to help them. Certainly government transfers are no long-run answer to poverty. Indeed, government transfers to the poor impede their economic improvement by convincing them that their well-being depends on what the state can do for them rather than on what they can do for themselves.[1]

The importance of instilling and maintaining a sense of responsibility in the poor cannot be overemphasized. But the connection between government transfers and responsible behavior by recipients is not the primary concern addressed here. Equally important in understanding the dismal record of transfer programs is the connection between these programs and responsible behavior by those who vote for them. Both the political popularity and guaranteed failure of government transfers are rooted in the fundamental irresponsibility of those who support these transfers with their votes. Contrary to the prevailing sentiment, voting for government attempts to

89

help the poor with transfers has less to do with compassion than with avoiding responsibility. The person who votes with a sense of both genuine responsibility and compassion will vote against government transfers as a means of helping the poor.

Under the best of circumstances it is difficult to help the poor. When help is given to those who find themselves in unfortunate situations, it necessarily lowers the cost of taking actions that lead into those situations, or lowers the benefit of taking actions that lead out of them. Charles Murray brilliantly illustrates this problem in his 1984 book *Losing Ground* when he discusses the considerable difficulty that would be encountered by a government program (even an extremely well-financed program) attempting to help people quit smoking. The problem of lowering the cost of becoming poor is one faced by any effort to help the poor, whether government or private. Private efforts at poverty relief have a tremendous advantage over government efforts, however, because the former benefit from a sense of responsibility on the part of both donors and recipients that is completely lacking in the case of the latter.

Indeed, a primary attraction of government welfare programs is that they largely eliminate the need for those who are paying for these programs to feel any real sense of responsibility for either the cost to themselves or the consequences to others, including the poor. Converting concern for the poor into a social responsibility (i.e., a responsibility that everyone should care about) makes it a concern for which almost no one feels any responsibility. This not only explains why public welfare has been so politically popular, it also goes a long way in explaining why it has been so counterproductive.

The Joint Responsibility of Private Charity

For reasons to be explained in the next section, the voluntary nature of contributions to private relief efforts both reflects and motivates a far greater willingness to assume responsibility for the cost and consequences of those contributions than when contributions are conscripted in response to majority voting. And because private charities tend to be locally focused and relatively small, it is far easier for those who contribute to them to observe the effectiveness of their contributions than when their contribution is taken by the Internal Revenue Service and buried in the federal budget.

There are other reasons why private relief organizations can be expected to behave more responsibly than public agencies. Private organizations compete with one another for donations they receive. Although it would be an exaggeration to say that most donors will go to the trouble to monitor the effectiveness of the private charities they contribute to, some will. Certainly a private charity has to be far more concerned that poor performance will result in its donors redirecting their generosity than does a public transfer agency.

Private relief organizations are not circumscribed, as are public agencies, by legal requirements to sort people into broad bureaucratically determined categories that prevent them from making subjective distinctions among recipients. Private organizations thus have far more latitude to make the age-old distinction between the deserving and undeserving poor. And because of the competition they face, private charities can be expected to act on that distinction. A private charity is strongly motivated to channel its funds to those who give evidence that they will use the aid to good advantage. Private charities reduce the opportunity for recipients to exploit the availability of transfers by substituting them for responsible efforts to help themselves. Furthermore, transfer recipients are more likely to experience a feeling of gratitude for help from a private gift than for a monthly check from an impersonal public agency. Help received through public agencies will tend to be viewed as a right that invokes no sense of gratitude or obligation from recipients. There is no surprise in the fact that so many public welfare recipients have become trapped in an intergenerational cycle of dependency.

It would be disingenuous to argue that private charity is a

perfect way of helping the poor. All attempts to help the poor are loaded with obstacles and there are no perfect ways. The advantage of private charity is that it does more to help the poor overcome poverty than do the public transfer programs. And the primary reason is that private charity engenders a sense of responsibility on the part of both donors and recipients. This joint responsibility is missing in the case of public transfers, and it is missing in a way that has gone completely unnoticed by those who have recognized the devastating effect public transfers have on recipient responsibility. The political mechanism through which public transfers are approved and implemented greatly lowers the level of responsibility exercised by those who pay for those transfers. This lack of donor responsibility is just as important in explaining the failure of public transfers as is the lack of recipient responsibility.

The Temptation to Vote Irresponsibly

Voting is an act of civic responsibility, and nothing written here denies that cornerstone of a democratic political order. At the same time a responsible discussion of voting requires an honest evaluation of its weaknesses, and the primary weakness of voting is that it encourages people to satisfy their expressive urges in ways that are often irresponsible. The problem lies in the arithmetic of voting.

Consider that in most elections the likelihood that the outcome will be decided by one vote is so small that it can be reasonably ignored. Your chances of being taken prisoner by space aliens on the way to the polls are only imperceptibly smaller than are your chances of determining the outcome of the election with your vote once (if) you get to the polls. This does not mean that your vote has no value unless it breaks what would otherwise be a tie. Your vote will always affect the size of the majority, and this can convey important information on the public mood to our elected representatives. But it does mean that people who are deciding (1) how informed to become on the issues, (2) whether to vote, and (3) how to vote, do so with at least an implicit understanding that their individual votes are not likely to be decisive.

The indecisiveness of an individual vote has significant implications for the temptation to vote with little sense of responsibility. Consider that all citizens stand to benefit from public policy guided by well-informed voters. For most people, however, significant costs are associated with becoming informed on the candidates and proposals at issue in an election. Each individual would find these costs worth incurring if incurring them was the only way he could receive the benefits from well informed public policy; i.e., if his vote was decisive. But because any one vote is so unlikely to make a difference, the payoff in terms of better policy from being an informed voter can be ignored by individual voters. Each voter knows that he will benefit from good public policy, regardless of whether or not he becomes informed, if enough other voters make informed choices at the polls. And even if others are not expected to become informed, each individual recognizes that becoming informed himself will have little effect on the quality of public policy. So unless an individual simply enjoys being informed for the sake of being informed, the temptation is strong to attempt to free-ride on the informed voting of others.

Of course, such free riding is hardly responsible behavior. If most people attempt to free-ride on the informed voting of others, there will not be much of a ride since public policy would be less informed than everyone would like to see. Yet the evidence suggests that voters do attempt, though rather unsuccessfully, to free-ride on the information others bring to the polls. Survey after survey finds that voters have very little information on the candidates and the proposals on which they are voting. This "rational ignorance" is the predictable consequence of the arithmetic of voting, but even so it reflects a great deal of irresponsibility on the part of voters. Because of this irresponsibility, voters are easily swayed by cosmetic considerations. Arguments that are superficially plausible and easy to understand are more effective at influencing voters than substantive, but subtle, arguments based on often complicated analysis.

A question naturally arises at this point. If individual voters have an insignificant effect on the outcome of elections, why aren't voter turnouts even lower than they are? If each voter recognizes that his vote is unlikely to be decisive, people must not go to the polls individually expecting to decisively promote their interests by voting. Clearly the cost of voting in terms of time alone is greater than the benefit an individual can expect to realize by influencing the election outcome with his vote. Something else has to be providing the primary motivation for voting.

The urge to express oneself in favor of things which one approves and against things which one disapproves is strong. People vote for much the same reason that they send get-well cards to friends, or cheer for the home team and jeer the opposing team in athletic contests. People don't send get-well cards to friends because they believe that their cards will determine whether their friends get well. Nor do people cheer for the home team because they believe that their cheer will make the difference between victory or defeat. Sending get-well cards and cheering for the home team provide the senders and cheerers the good feeling that comes from expressing support for people and activities they feel are important. Voting provides people the same opportunity to feel good about themselves for expressing support for things that they feel are worthy.

Expressive voting can reflect a sense of duty on the part of people to participate in the electoral process and make their voices heard regardless of how much effect any one vote may have. To the extent that responsibility really is being reflected here, and that it also motivates people to become informed and public-spirited voters, such expressive voting is to be applauded. But unfortunately expressive voting allows uninformed voters to capture small individual gains by voting in ways that impose large collective costs. In particular, voting can provide an opportunity for individuals to feel compassionate at low cost by expressing themselves in favor of expensive government programs that claim to reduce poverty while actually harming the poor.

To illustrate, consider a voter's response to a government transfer program justified as necessary for reducing poverty under the assumption that he is rationally ignorant of the harmful effect the program is likely to have on the poor. If the voter is at all typical, he has been brought up to feel that he should be sympathetic to the plight of the poor, and therefore to feel good about himself if he does things to help the poor, such as (at least in his mind) voting for government transfer programs (or for those political candidates who favor such programs). To make our illustration as forceful as possible, assume that the voter is fully aware that if the proposal passes it will impose a cost on him of say, $1,000 as a taxpayer, which is far greater than the value he is willing to pay for the feeling of virtue he can realize from voting in favor of the proposal, say 25 cents.[2] The question is: Will he vote for or against the proposal?

At first the answer may seem obvious. He will not likely make a private charitable contribution of $1,000 to help the poor if the satisfaction from making the contribution is worth only 25 cents, unless he is an unusually compassionate person. But there is an important difference between making a private charitable contribution and voting in favor of an equally costly public transfer. And because of this difference, the individual, who would donate only a small amount privately, may vote to donate a large amount publicly.

The decision to make a private donation is decisive. The individual who "votes" to donate $1,000 privately incurs an unequivocal cost of $1,000. He incurs the cost with 100 percent certainty if he votes to make the donation and avoids the cost with 100 percent certainty if he votes not to make the dona-

tion. On the other hand, the decision to favor a public donation at the polls is not at all decisive, since an individual vote is
not likely to affect the outcome of the election. Voting in favor
of a government transfer program makes an individual only
imperceptibly more likely to incur his share of the required tax
cost than if he votes against the program. The cost to the individual of voting for a proposal that will cost him $1,000 if it
passes is equal to $1,000 X (times) the probability that the vote
of everyone else is evenly split. For reasons already discussed,
this probability is extremely low.

To continue the illustration, assume the probability that the
individual's vote is decisive is equal to 1/20,000, which for elections on federal and state issues is far larger than the probability that the outcome will be decided by one vote. But with this
probability it follows that the expected cost to the individual of
voting in favor of the proposal is only $1,000/20,000, or 5
cents. Since the voter values the feeling of virtue he will receive
from casting a favorable vote at 25 cents, it makes sense from
his perspective to vote yes. Voting in this case, and in many
other cases, allows people to express their superior virtue, and
therefore feel good about themselves, at low cost and little
sense of responsibility for the consequences of what they are
voting for.[3]

Forgetting the Poor

A good gauge of the real commitment to helping the poor
on the part of those who vote in favor of public transfer programs is what they do after they walk out of the voting booth
feeling good about themselves. If government transfers are to
have any hope of actually helping the poor, it takes a lot more
than just transferring more money into the public sector.
Poverty programs would have to be designed with extreme
care to avoid the problems of dependency already discussed.
Once the programs were properly designed they would have to

be implemented in ways that put the long-run interest of the poverty reduction ahead of short-run political concerns. Such design and implementation would take the ongoing involvement of citizens whose commitment to the poor goes far beyond making a low-cost expression of generosity at the polls. Yet how many, after voting in favor of transfer programs at the polls, go to the considerable time and expense to work for effective poverty programs? Very few. With rare exceptions those who express concern for the poor at the polls afterward spend more time watching toothpaste commercials on television than with direct political action to make sure the tax dollars they voted for actually help the poor.

There will be plenty of people, however, who do devote significant time to influencing government transfer policy. But few of these people will be motivated by an overriding concern for the poor. When people become actively involved politically, it is typically for the purpose of obtaining private benefits, not to promote broad social objectives such as poverty reduction. This is not to say that people never take political action to improve public policy. Obviously they do. But working for better public policy is the same as contributing to a public good, such as national defense, and the rationale for having government force people to contribute to such goods is that individuals have little motivation to do so voluntarily. If people could be depended upon to work for general social objectives with the same dedication that they do to secure private advantage, there would be little rationale for the coercive powers of government.

Large numbers of politically organized groups have strong interests in government transfer programs justified in the name of helping the poor. These groups are invariably organized around occupational interests, and benefit from government poverty programs by administering them, consulting for them, and supplying products it is argued the poor should have but would not buy (at least in sufficient quantities) even if they had the necessary income. These groups include social welfare professionals, academic researchers, consulting firms, farm organizations, construction associations and unions, medical associations, university organizations, the public school establishment, and many others. Although these groups always lobby by claiming great concern for helping the poor, they are able to benefit from expanding and altering transfer programs that do little to help the poor, and often harm them.[4]

Whenever money is transferred through the political process, a competition ensues between different interest groups for that money, and the result of that competition depends far more on the relative political influence of the competing groups than on the rhetoric of public-spirited concern and compassion that accompanies the competition. This is a straightforward observation that only those with the most romantic notions of the political process would challenge. Yet the implication of this observation for the ability of government to help the poor through redistribution programs is profoundly at variance with the prevailing wisdom.

The prevailing wisdom is that government can, and should, help the poor by altering the distribution of income generated by market competition.[5] But Newt Gingrich is right and the prevailing wisdom is wrong. The problem with government redistribution to the poor is not just that the poor's sense of responsibility and community is undermined by the visible transfer they receive, but that on balance the government does not redistribute anything to the poor.

The crucial question here is, are there any reasons for believing that the poor possess skills that allow them to do better in political competition than in market competition? I have never heard anyone who recommends government programs to help the poor ask this question, much less answer it in the affirmative. But unless the poor are somehow more skilled at political than market competition, there is no reason for believing that increasing the share of the national income allocated through the political process can help the poor by reducing income inequality. It is true that the poor receive visible government transfers. But it is also true that the poor pay for numerous and expensive transfers that go to the non-poor. They do so through taxes many of which are buried in the prices paid by the poor), higher prices (agricultural price supports hit the poor particularly hard), denied opportunities for employment (many examples can be found in occupational licensing and regulation), and other ways, all of which are less visible than the transfers they receive. The poor are "out-competed" in the political arena just as they are in the marketplace.[6]

The evidence is clearly consistent with the proposition that government transfer programs have failed to alter the distribution of income in favor of the poor. Several studies that look at the distribution of income over the last several decades (spanning the period during which government greatly increased its transfer activities) have found that, after adjusting for taxes and transfers, the income distribution has not significantly changed one way or the other. This failure of redistribution efforts has been recognized even by those who are sympathetic to government transfer programs for helping the poor, once they have examined the evidence. Having examined the recent studies on changes in the distribution of income, Robert Haveman, a poverty researcher at the University of Wisconsin, has concluded, "In spite of massive increases in federal government taxes and spending, we are about as unequal in 1988 as we were in 1950....By 1988, those at the end of the income line had not moved closer to the middle, expensive efforts notwithstanding."[7]

Unfortunately, the situation for the poor is worse than is suggested by ineffective government redistribution programs. Even if government programs were on balance redistributing income to the poor, it would not follow that the poor would be benefiting from the programs. General economic growth is adversely affected by government transfers as they reduce productive incentives for both those who pay for them and those who receive them. So unless government transfers increased the share of national income going to the poor by more than they decreased national income, the poor end up absolutely worse off. Given the evidence that government transfers do not increase the share of the economic pie going to the poor, the inescapable conclusion is that these transfers have made the poor worse off in terms of the money they receive. And this ignores the sense of responsibility and self-esteem lost when the money received comes from the efforts of others rather than from one's own efforts. This is by far the greatest loss the poor have suffered at the hands of government "compassion."

Real Compassion

The best way to help the poor is by reducing the scope of negative-sum political activity—not by "reinventing" government but by reimposing serious constraints on government. To accomplish this, however, requires jettisoning the seductive notion that government is the best vehicle for exercising our feeling of compassion. Most compassion exercised through the political process is a cheap imitation of the real thing and is invariably subverted by powerful interest groups. The people who display real compassion for the poor are those who assume the responsibility to (1) donate to private relief efforts and (2) resist the temptation of cheap virtue by voting against all redistribution schemes (and the politicians who support them) no matter how compassionate these schemes are claimed to be.

Notes

[1]Hillsdale College President George Roche made this point in 1971 when he observed, "The individual who is relieved of responsibility for his own actions incurs the gravest possible handicap for the future development of his own personality. Soon such men find no capacity in themselves, and

turn to government for the solution of all problems." See George Roche, *Frederic Bastiat: A Man Alone* (New Rochelle, N.Y.: Arlington House, 1971), 162–63.

[2]The choice of 25 cents is not to suggest that people place such a small value on the sense of virtue that comes from efforts to help the unfortunate. The value is chosen to emphasize the point that people will often vote for proposals that provide them with a sense of virtue even when the cost of the program is high and the value of the sense of virtue is low.

[3]For a detailed discussion of the broad political implications of the tendency for people to attach little weight to the consequences of the propositions they favor at the polls, see Geoffrey Brennan and Loren Lomasky, *Democracy and Decision: The Pure Theory of Electoral Preference* (Cambridge: University of Cambridge Press, 1993).

[4]For a detailed discussion of how lobbying by organized interest groups in the name of helping the poor actually harms the poor, see chapter 8 of Dwight R. Lee and Richard B. McKenzie, *Failure and Progress: The Bright Side of the Dismal Science* (Washington, DC: Cato Institute, 1993).

[5]For example, a recent article in The *Economist* stated, "The collapse of communism may have proved Adam Smith's invisible hand to be a superior economic engine, but it is one that is still morally suspect to many who worry that economic rewards are not being shared adequately. For the market economy has no moral sensibility....[V]oters who feel uncomfortable about homeless people on the streets may choose to sacrifice some growth to reduce income inequalities. That is a valid political choice." See "Inequality," The *Economist*, November 5, 1994: 19–21.

[6]The great nineteenth-century French economist and philosopher Frederic Bastiat pointed out long ago that the poor are not advantaged by political competition. In his words, "When, under the pretext of fraternity, the legal code imposes mutual sacrifices on the citizens, human nature is not thereby abrogated. Everyone will then direct his efforts toward contributing little to, and taking much from, the common fund of sacrifices. Now, is it the most unfortunate who gain in this struggle? Certainly not, but rather the most influential and calculating." See Roche, op cit., 88.

[7]See Robert Haveman, *Starting Even: An Equal Opportunity Program to Combat the Nation's New Poverty* (New York: Simon and Schuster, 1988), 121.

Gordon Tullock

Whose Welfare?

Social Security as Welfare

The "welfare state" is the name most people use to describe the current plethora of government programs aimed at helping the poor and the downtrodden. But they often forget that the biggest—and most expensive—program of the welfare state is actually Social Security. Established by the U.S. government during the Depression Era of the 1930s, this program has become a compulsory and heavy burden for the millions of working citizens who pay for it.

Social Security recipients are not necessarily poor—indeed, in some years, their average income is higher than that of the younger people who are paying taxes to support them. My own case is a good example. I have an endowed chair at a university. I have made some fortunate investments. I am not married. I don't have children. Therefore, I qualify as "wealthy." But even when I am 72 years old, I can still work and draw my pension.

Who Really Pays?

Ironically, the old-age pension system and the medical care government provides for the elderly were actually invented by Germany's Prince Otto von Bismarck (1815–1898), who rarely championed the cause of the poor and the aged. The program he invented has spread, in one form or another, throughout the world. The U.S. system is funded by a payroll tax on workers, also inspired by Bismarck. A brilliant politician, he conceived of the idea of telling people that half of this tax is paid for by the employee and half of it is paid for by the employer. Of course, in reality, the entire tax is paid for by the employee; it is money *he would have received as a part of his salary* that is the source of the employer's "share." Most people don't really think about where the money comes from and are thus easily deceived. This is also because the Social Security Administration goes out of its way to hide the truth and continually refers to the employer's share as if it were "found money."

The same is true for medical insurance, which in many cases is another disguised form of welfare. President Clinton's proposed health care reform program that was stalled in 1994 was going to do Bismarck one better and say that 80 percent of medical costs would be paid for by the employer. But, of course 100 percent would have been paid by the employee. As an employee, you are only hired if your contribution to the organization is more valuable than its total cost and that cost includes all payroll taxes.

For most of the population, the Social Security tax is proportional to income at roughly 15 percent. As income gets higher and higher, the tax is capped. In my case, some time about the middle of the year, my nominal pay goes up sharply because I have already paid the full amount the government will collect from me for Social Security, and, therefore, it no longer deduct a sum from my paycheck. This makes the tax regressive—the most regressive tax of all.

When Social Security was first inaugurated, the amount that an individual received as a pension was largely controlled by the amount that he had paid in. This was then changed so that the pension did not rise as fast as his employed income in the later part of his working life. Recently the government has begun putting a tax on the income an individual derives from Social Security. These two changes have made the whole system less regressive than it used to be, although it may still be regarded as a highly regressive income transfer in which people like me do better than people with average incomes.

The Coming Deficit

Social Security payments to today's retirees are currently covered by Social Security taxes on today's workers, but this may change in the future. Predictions about what will happen thirty or forty years hence are always difficult, but it seems unlikely that young people now entering the labor force will receive anywhere near as much in pension payments as they would receive had they saved the same amount of money, invested it, and bought annuities. There is an element of risk involved, but Social Security is also risky.

Just look at the immediate problems elsewhere in the world. A number of Latin American countries, for example, have been forced to slash their pension programs so that individuals now retired are only getting ten percent of their legally stipulated pensions. When our government has been confronted with such crises in the past, it has, in general, taken a different route: raising taxes and continuing to pay out the pensions. Note that I said "in general." There have been several cases in which the cost-of-living adjustment has been skipped for a year, which lowers the rates, and there have been some minor technical changes in the rule which leaves the rate somewhat lower for certain people. Nevertheless, raising taxes always seems to have been the preferred option.

Demographers worry about the problem that the population of the United States is getting older. Modern medicine is keeping people alive longer. The birth rate is low. We are not even replacing ourselves. Thus the number of workers who will be available to pay the taxes to support each individual pensioner is falling and is predicted to fall very sharply in the next century. Demographic predictions of the past have been fre-

quently wrong, but if this one is correct, the taxes necessary to
support the pension program will indeed be extremely high.

Some years ago, Congress became worried about the predicted Social Security deficit and passed a law that raised payroll taxes steeply to higher levels than ever before. The idea
was to establish a trust fund to cover the future shortfall. But
the trust fund was not a cure-all; in fact, it will be exhausted in
fifteen years.

The trust fund is invested entirely in government bonds and
then the money is spent. So taxpayers will have to pay additional funds in the next century, just as they would if there
were no trust fund at all. The only difference is that part of
their taxes will be used to repay the government bonds with the
money then being used for the pensions, rather than all of it
going directly to pensions. This method—of taxing current
employees in order to buy government bonds with the money
then spent—means a good deal of our current government
expenditures are actually being financed by our most regressive tax. In years past, Senator Moynihan (D-NY) proposed that
this project be eliminated by simply stopping the trust fund
and reducing the taxes proportionately. This would make the
apparent government deficit larger than it is now, and might
require either economies or an enactment of other taxes. The
Democratically-controlled Congress not only rejected his proposal but refused to give it serious consideration.

A Regressive Tax

There are other aspects of the Social Security program that
are even more regressive. Look, for example, at the way we
treat the very poor. One recent major study reveals that we
have made very little historical progress in the "War on
Poverty." In the 1850s, programs for the poor guaranteed
about the same percentage of average incomes as programs in
the 1990s. The "working poor" are particularly hard-hit. They
pay the full Social Security tax on everything they earn. When

they find themselves in financial need, they are enrolled in a government welfare program like Supplementary Security Income (SSI) that pays them just about what they would have received if they had never paid any taxes at all. Indeed, they are paid the same as those who did not make any Social Security contributions. They pay taxes all their lives, and 15 percent out of their small income feels like a pretty big chunk. And when they leave the workforce, their retirement payments are the same as if had they not contributed one red cent. This takes regressiveness to an extreme.

Diversifying Risk

The non-poor worker faces serious challenges, too. In practice, it seems likely that when an individual has nothing but risky alternatives, the most sensible thing he can do is to try and diversify his risk. Thus having part of his planning for old age handled by the government and part handled by his savings is a good idea. There are two other things he can do to diversify, one of which is to have children who probably will take care of him when he is old, and the other is to plan on taking "light" jobs that will pay at least something when he is old, thus getting four potential sources of revenue for his remaining years.

In the past, there were all sorts of specialized light jobs that were available to senior citizens, and generally the people who took them could support themselves reasonably well. It seems to me that, on the whole, people planning for their old age should assume that Social Security will only serve as part of their income.

The Prospects for Reform

The problem with Social Security today is that it is an old-fashioned "Ponzi scheme." The old-age pensions of those individuals who have them and those approaching old age who expect to have them, are entirely dependent upon current taxes. Dropping the scheme would mean that thousands of people who have been promised by politicians that they could depend on Social Security would be betrayed. On the other hand, if we decide to continue paying those pensions, there is no source of revenue except taxes on the younger generation. And if we are terminating the plan in the future, let us say in 20 years, those citizens would get nothing back.

From the standpoint of Prince Bismarck in Germany in the 1870s and the New Dealers in the United States in the 1930s, Social Security was politically profitable. As it started, it provided a great benefit for huge numbers of older people who had not made tax payments during their lives. And there was that misleading nonsense about the employer's "share" that seemed so attractive an idea. In the 1990s, the truth is finally coming out. Social Security was, and is, too good to be true. In the not-too-distant future, individuals will actually pay more for their pension in total than they would if they had invested the money at ordinary interest rates.

How do we get out of what appears to be an untenable situation? My guess is that the American people won't make major reforms voluntarily. At some point, the program will break down, and a great many people will be injured. Then, and only then, will there be a chance to set up an alternative system in which we will no longer make no general payments to the elderly, only payments to those whose income falls below some minimum level. Since most retirees are not poor, the total cost to taxpayers will be relatively low, and the regressive nature of the system will be eliminated.

Learning from the Past

We will also take a serious look at what has worked in the past. In the 1920s, there were regular programs, mainly paid for and administered by local governments, churches, and private charities, to take care of those individuals who were unable to take care of themselves. These were usually administered on by officials who knew the aid recipients personally or who at least had the opportunity to make sure the recipients were truly in need of assistance. And there was a regular procedure for taking care of older people in the form of extended families and municipally-supported retirement homes.

The standard of living was not very high for most citizens in the early part of the twentieth century—it certainly couldn't compare with the standard enjoyed today. But people could count on a far more personal, more reliable safety net, at a very low tax cost. They would have abhorred the idea of welfare for the middle class, which is what Social Security has become. Their way of life may have been more modest, but it provided strong incentives for getting and keeping a job and for saving money. We need such incentives. Without them, it isn't just Social Security that will be bankrupt; it is our society.

A Viable Alternative to Other Forms of Welfare: "Workfare"

The ideas I have advanced about Social Security apply to every program of the welfare state. When it comes to "general assistance," we should provide some kind of minimum income to the poorest members of society only. And welfare recipients in good health should be required to work for their government checks. An individual choosing between $7,000 a year as relief payment without any work requirement, and an honest job at $9,000, might well choose $7,000. If you make him work, he is more likely take the job at $9,000, or indeed any amount over $7,000. There is another advantage. If we did this, we could raise the minimum income which we guarantee, and there would be fewer "welfare loafers."

But "workfare" is not easy to implement. It is difficult and complex in the extreme. Imagine you are running a government workfare program. You must anticipate that you will receive on any given day the applications of an uncertain number of people who have lost their jobs or for another reason have no suitable income, and you are going to have to find them a job immediately. You might take inspiration from the former Soviet government. The U.S.S.R. had a constitutional provision that guaranteed that the state would provide everyone with a job. If an individual turned up unemployed, he was put to work picking up litter in Moscow's parks, or employment was "arranged" for him in Siberia. This last option is not as unusual as it sounds: For a long time, Sweden offered something very similiar. If you showed up at the employment exchange and said you were unemployed and wanted relief, the authorities would respond: "It is very fortunate, Mr. Swenson, that we have a number of openings cutting lumber in Lapland. Here is an introduction to one of the companies that hires that kind of labor." As a result, Sweden had very few registered unemployed.

In the United States, under a workfare system, you would have to expect a lot of people turning up without warning because a plant closing or a recession. You would, as I indicated, need to find jobs for them without delay, and these jobs would have to meet a number of stringent conditions. The first of these is that they must require no particular skill. This is not because the people who become unemployed are all lacking in skill but because they have different types of skill. The second condition is that these jobs would have to be extremely flexible. There would be no telling when a worker would start or quit and move on to a new job. And he would need to be free to take time off for other job interviews. The third condition is that the jobs must be easy to monitor. You would not want to maintain a large expensive supervisory staff who would be idle when the unemployed were scarce and overworked when they were numerous.

These conditions, hard as they are, *can* be met, even by something as simple as trash collection. As I have already pointed out, this form of workfare was devised in the Soviet Union. Perhaps communism had one good lesson to teach us after all. But picking up litter is not the only option; there are others. We need to identify them, and once we have, we should put the full force of American public opinion behind them.

Richard E. Wagner

Progress, Poverty, and Democracy

In the late nineteenth century, two prominent economists, William Stanley Jevons and Henry George, articulated their thoughts on the relationship between poverty and progress. In a 1869 address to the Manchester Statistical Society, Jevons lamented how medical charities "nourish in the poorest classes a contented sense of dependence on the richer classes for those ordinary requirements of life which they ought to be led to provide for themselves." He continued, "We cannot be supposed yet to have reached a point at which the public or private charity of one class towards another can be dispensed with, but I do think we ought to look towards such a state of things. True progress will tend to render every class self-reliant and independent."[1] In Jevons's judgment, the elimination of poverty and dependence is a natural outcome of a progressive market economy. This is not to deny that people may be hit by misfortune not of their making or may make bad choices on their own. It is only to claim that within a market economy people will develop a network of practices, organizations, and institutions that will elevate wealth and autonomy over poverty and dependence.

On the other side of the Atlantic a decade later, Henry George published his argument in a book that is still famous today: *Progress and Poverty*.[2] In sharp contrast to Jevons, George claimed that progress itself is actually the main source of poverty because it leads to increasing rents for landowners and decreasing purchasing power for those who are forced to live by their labor alone. His radical solution was the elimination of all private land ownership.

As an empirical matter, concerns about poverty are clearly robust today. This surely would not surprise Henry George, who could point to the continued existence of private owner-ship of land as the reason for poverty in the midst of progress. Moreover Stanley Jevons was enough of an empiricist to acknowledge that self-reliance and independence had not grown as steadily as he had thought they would. Poverty occu-pies a solid place on the agenda of contemporary discourse, and by most measures its incidence has changed little over the past generation.[3] It would seem as though Henry George was a more accurate forecaster than William Stanley Jevons. But has the course of history validated George and refuted Jevons?

We know, of course, that empirical observations never explain themselves. Explanation requires the aid of some con-ceptual framework. When such a framework is supplied, it is possible to reconcile the contemporary persistence of poverty with a recognition that Jevons was right about progress and George was wrong. Any explanation of the relation between progress and poverty must assume that other relevant influ-ences on that relationship stay the same. But there are other relevant influences that have changed in the period since Jevons wrote. In particular, the character of our political sys-tem has changed dramatically, and it has moved in a direction that fosters poverty and dependence. Jevons took for granted the continuation of some form of liberal democratic state, where the state is principally concerned with protecting peo-ple from each other so that people can pursue freely their cho-sen projects. He did not anticipate the emergence of the social democratic state, where the state is an arena within which per-sonal rights and liabilities are continually being brokered. Had we continued to live within a regime of liberal democracy, the truth of the Jevonian vision would have been plain to see. The social democratic state, however, follows a different logic, one that dampens progress and encourages dependence. This, anyway, is the thesis I seek to advance.

Liberal Democracy vs. Social Democracy

In his widely noted book on *The End of History and the Last Man*, Francis Fukuyama asserts that we have arrived at the very end of Hegelian history, in that we have now seen the universal and eternal triumph of liberal democracy.[4] The liberal component of this triumph results because only market economics deliver the goods. This century has shown conclusively the failures of collectivist economies. The democratic component involves the claim that only democracies can provide the recognition that men require, as recognition achieved among equals is more satisfying than recognition achieved among unequals. Hence, liberal democracy stands at the end of history, simply because there is no alternative.

While I have great admiration for liberal democracy, I find Fukuyama's argument to founder on an inadequate taxonomy, i.e., order of classification. The dramatic changes that we have observed over the past generation or two do not illustrate the ascendancy of liberal democracy. Rather they illustrate the metamorphosis of liberal democracy into social democracy, along with a failure to keep our language consistent with our practice. To cite the retreat of Society-style socialism and Franco-style authoritarianism as evidence for the triumph of liberal democracy is to adopt an unduly narrow view of historical options that ignores the currently robust alternative of social democracy. It is surely social democracy, as a kinder and gentler form of socialism than that which characterized the Soviet empire, that seems to be the popular path these days. Moreover, this is a path that is easy to catch, and once caught is difficult to leave.[5]

Liberal democracy and social democracy are easy to distinguish in terms of principle. The difference between the two is essentially the difference between living in a society where relationships and institutions are grounded in *private property* and one where they are grounded in *common property*.[6] Liberal democracy reflects the premise that people and their rights of person and property precede government, which leads to the formulation articulated in our first constitutional document, the Declaration of Independence, that governments exist to secure those prior individual rights. Government is a reflection of people's use of their rights, and is not a source of rights.[7] Liberal democracy adopts the orientation that people can do as they choose without requiring state permission, provided only that they do not abridge the similar rights of other people in the process. Liberal democracy is the political activity of a people whose conduct and relationships with one another is governed by the principles of private property, contract, and free association.

Social democracy represents an opposing orientation: Government is the source of rights, and people may do individually only what the state allows them to do. In a social democracy, collective judgments trump individual rights. To be sure, practical considerations relating to the inability of legislatures to be involved in everything will ensure some scope for individual autonomy. The reach of the legislature is limited in practice, but there is no limitation based on principle. Social democracy is the political activity of people whose conduct is governed by the principles of common property, with the state serving as the arena within which access to the commons is dispensed. The course of movement over much of this century has surely been a movement from private property to common property, from liberal democracy to social democracy. We have arrived at the point in the "Land of the Free" where you must often seek the state's permission before you can cut trees, build fences, move soil, create ponds, construct buildings, or to engage in any of any immense variety of commercial activities. What we are now living under is more of a system of economic organization within a regulated commons than a system of economic organization based on private property and free markets.

Policy Analysis in Constitutional Perspective

The collapse of the socialist economics has surely been responsible for some of the renewed interest in the scholarship of Ludwig von Mises and Friedrich A. Hayek in particular, as well as Austrian economics generally.[8] Mises and Hayek explained why a system of central economic planning can never secure coordination among the participants in the economic process. The extent of knowledge that would be necessary is too vast and detailed for anyone to begin to accumulate. A complex economy is an orderly network of self-organized relationships that could never be organized in hierarchical fashion as a goal-centered organization.[9] There is no option to a self-organized polyarchy, i.e., "government by the many," though it is possible for government intervention to warp, distort, and impede the operation of those self-organizing processes.[10]

For the most part, the conventional approach to the economic analysis of the public sphere treats public policies as interventions into the economy that create outcomes desired by state officials—outcomes that would not be generated through market processes. Rather than one massive plan, there is a miscellaneous collection of state policies imposed onto what would otherwise have been a market economy. State policies thus treat market outcomes as a first draft that is then revised by those policies to achieve state-sponsored ends. The ability of those policies truly to achieve their objectives requires the same ability to plan without markets that full-scale planning requires, even if a smaller scale of planning is involved. For policy measures that are designed to achieve specific objectives, compared with measures designed simply to facilitate transactions, can be successful only if there exist no unanticipated or unintended consequences, which in turn is possible only if state officials possess the detailed knowledge that no one can possess.

The standard approach to policy analysis also fails to recognize that policy formation is itself subject to an economic logic that links and unifies the array of particular policy measures.[11] That economic logic characterizes the enactment of particular policy measures as reflecting the pursuit of political gain through a particular constitutional framework. Ordinary economic logic describes investment as flowing to different activities so as to equalize returns at the different margins of investment. That logic applied to politics describes policies as pursued so as to equalize political support across the various policy margins. This statement is very formal, to be sure, but it leads us to recognize that the type of policy measure that is enacted will depend on the costs and gains that legislators anticipate securing from its enactment. Those costs and gains, moreover, will depend on the constitutional setting within which policies are crafted, which, in turn, implies that the pattern of legislation will develop differently under alternative constitutional systems.[12]

A system of liberal democracy offers a different constitutional setting for the operation of the entire array of policy markets than does a system of social democracy. Liberal democracy involves a government of limited powers, where there are wide avenues of life that simply cannot be touched by public policy. Social democracy involves no principled limitation on the reach of public policy. Limits will exist in practice, of course, but these will be defined in terms of the disinterest of political authorities on the one hand and the ability of people to evade or resist those authorities on the other hand. In a social democracy grounded in politics as the arena for the regulation of the commons, people compete over access to the commons. The same general economic principles operate in these political markets that operate in ordinary economic markets, just as the same economic principles operate in common property settings as operate in private property settings. Only the specific consequences differ as between the settings. To explore the impact of politics on poverty, it is necessary to ask how the replacement of a system of liberal democracy with one of social democracy is likely to affect the relationship between progress and poverty.

Politics and Poverty in a Social Democracy

The transformation of a system of liberal democracy into one of social democracy undermines the poverty-eroding, autonomy-strengthening features of liberal democracy. First of all, in its transformation of private property into common property, a system of social democracy lowers the rate of economic progress, thereby leading to a lower level of economic well-being in general. This general retardation of economic progress follows pretty much automatically from the comparative logic of common and private property that was well known to Aristotle and which has not been modified significantly in the subsequent millennia. The greater the extent to which economic life is organized through common property arrangements, the slower will be the rate of progress through time and the lower the level of economic well being at any one time.

Besides this general diminution in the force of economic progress within a society, a social democracy also promotes a shift of effort away from activities that are truly creative and productive into activities that retard the productive activities of others, as economist Gordon Tullock has explained in his theory of rent seeking.[13] Rather than seeking to produce that better mousetrap, and securing the gains of temporary monopoly as a reward, people will shift their efforts into such things as securing restrictions on the ability of other producers to operate with home-based labor, lobbying for tariffs, and campaigning for restrictions on the use of rodent poisons, to mention just three of the almost innumerable possibilities.

As compared with liberal democracy, a system of social democracy offers greater political profit for policy measures that promote poverty and dependence. A system of social democracy creates two sets of people who have interests that support the maintenance of poverty and dependence to a greater extent than would be true under liberal democracy. One set is the recipients of state-supported services, who are content with the terms of the trade by which they replace independence with state support and who might offer their voting support in return.[14] The other set is the providers of those services, for whom the continuation of poverty and dependence is a source of income. To be sure, this general setting characterizes commercial activities as well. A continued interest by people in the condition of their teeth and gums works to the advantage of dentists. However, dentists have to attract business in a setting where customers can choose freely to spend their money elsewhere, and where other people are free to invent substitutes for dental care. Unlike dentists, or anyone else in the private sector, public sector agencies do not have customers in the traditional sense. Those agencies do not receive their funds directly from customers who are free to use their funds elsewhere. Instead, they receive them from legislative committees whose members are generally self-selected for a particularly strong interest in the activities they oversee. For instance, there are a variety of employment agencies and mental health counselors who provide services on the market that are similar to some of those that are provided through government. In the private sector, however, the individuals who pay are the customers. The suppliers of those services must repeatedly convince the customers that the services they are buying are worthwhile. A health counselor who provided no remedy but sought simply to corral the largest clientele possible might succeed because perfection exists nowhere.

There are, however, systematic reasons why such conduct would have stronger survival value within the common property framework of a social democracy. In place of the direct competition for consumer dollars, where every consumer is potentially a marginally relevant consumer, there is a political process of budgetary appropriation. Within a private property setting, what is not spent is returned to owners. But in the common property setting of social democracy, such residual claimacy is absent. What is not spent simply reverts to the commons for grazing by others.[15] The public sector counterpart of the councilor faces a legislative committee whose members are generally relatively high demanders of the services being provided. The lack of residual claimacy will lead to less effectiveness in the delivery of services, which implies lower rates of remedy than would result within a regime of private property and market competition.

Moreover, it is inadequate to assess the impact of social democracy on poverty and dependence with reference to what are called "anti-poverty programs" alone. In assessing the transformation from liberal democracy to social democracy, it is necessary to consider the full consequences of a shift from a government of limited and enumerated powers to one of unlimited powers. A social democracy grounded in common property will play out differently along numerous dimensions than a system of liberal democracy grounded in private property. Any assessment of politics and poverty must take into account all of those dimensions. In this respect there is no good reason to think that the poor will gain more access to the commons, as compared to the access they could secure under liberal democracy, let alone achieve the greater access that might offset the general retardation of economic progress that social democracy would create. As just one example, what is called corporate welfare is as much a product of social democracy as is the traditional programs of the welfare state, most of which in turn benefit primarily members of the middle class.[16]

Constitutional Principle and the Fallacy
of the Mixed Economy

While I would never want to underestimate the tenacity of entrenched interests in politics, I do think there is also significant intellectual error that has helped to fuel the transformation from a limited system of liberal democracy to an unlimited system of social democracy. An important piece of that error resides in the construct of the mixed economy, and was reflected as well in Fukuyama's confounding of liberal and social democracy, which is the same thing as confounding capitalism and socialism. The doctrine of the "mixed economy" holds that we are neither capitalist nor socialist, but some mixture of both. This is not the case. As Walter Eucken notes in particular, there are two principles of economic organization, although there can be various illustrations of each principle.[17] A truly liberal democracy must entail a commitment to the principles of property and contract as organizing principles that are suitable for a self-organized society whose individual members have their own purposes, and where the state itself has no purpose that does not derive from the consent of the governed.

If the socialist principles of social democracy are injected into a liberal democracy, institutional inconsistency or incongruence is created. Consider some aspects of the provision of health care in a mixed economy in relation to its provision in an economy organized under the market principles of property, contract, and liability. In market economy, people will get what they pay for, in one way or another. It would be possible to imagine a setting where all choices concerning medical matters were made within market-generated institutions. There would, of course, be a wide variety of practices and organizations that would populate such a market. The provision of medical care would be essentially the same as the provision of any other service. A variety of insurance programs would arise as part of the market process, as no doubt would numerous charitable organizations. People would invest in new technology, including life-extension technology, to the extent they thought people would be willing to pay for those services.

Medical care would not be a "right" of any kind. The budget constraint that is inherent in life would apply as strongly to medical care as to anything else. Someone who would otherwise die without a heart transplant or without having a malignant tumor removed could secure that procedure only by convincing someone to supply that procedure. The means of securing agreement could be the simple payment of a market price. It could also be through participation in an insurance program (itself organized in conformity with market principles), or by securing support from a charitable provider (also organized in conformity with market principle). In any event, budget constraints are unavoidable and will limit the number of procedures performed.

Life and death would be matters of personal choice and ability to pay within the framework of a market economy, as would the quality of medical care generally. Similarly, people who engage in risky occupations, dangerous leisure time activities, or unhealthy lifestyles would bear the medical costs associated with those personal choices. If people who ride motorcycles incur higher medical costs on average than people who do not, they will bear the higher costs. If people who smoke incur higher medical costs, they will bear those costs. The provision of medical care within the framework offered by the principles of property, contract, and liability does nothing to undermine support for liberal principles.

In contrast, the collective provision of medical care in a way that violates the principles of property, contract, and liability can easily create political incentives that undermine personal liberty. Consider some of the recent controversies concerning life styles and the costs of health care, particularly those concerning the smoking of cigarettes and the drinking of alcoholic beverages. In a market economy, these lifestyle choices are personal matters. The actuarial evidence shows that people who smoke have lower average life expectancies than nonsmokers, though there are many smokers who lead long lives and nonsmokers who die early. Insurance within a market economy would charge people in different risk categories different prices that would reflect, in a competitive market, the different costs of providing service.

With collective provision, however, this changes, at least so long as collective provision does not conform to the central principles of property, contract, and liability. Suppose medical care is financed through state budgets, or, equivalently, through private insurance restricted by government to charge common pricing. Once this happens, a new network of interests is created. People who make relatively low use of a service form a natural interest group, whose members have interests that are opposed to those who might make relatively high use. What was once a matter of a simple toleration of difference choices of lifestyles under conditions where the choosers bear the costs associated with their choices, becomes a matter of political concern. In the presence of collective provision or common pricing, activities that entail above-average costs, actuarially speaking, will be shifted partially onto those whose activities entail below-average costs. The transfer of medical care from a market-based to a collective-based mode of organization generates pressures for a similar transfer of control regarding a variety of other personal choices.

The state necessarily becomes a battleground for the adjudication of disputes over personal lifestyles; the commons creates a battleground over which contests for access are inescapable. When economic activity is organized according to the principles of property, contract, and liability, a society can tolerate peaceably a variety of such lifestyles because those who conduct more costly patterns of life pay for them. But once the market principle of personal responsibility is abridged for some principle of collective responsibility, interest groups are automatically established that will bring personal lifestyles onto the political agenda.

Capitalism, with its principle of personal responsibility, does not blend with socialism and its principle of collective responsibility. An institutional framework represented by the principles of property, contract, and liability is a capitalistic framework for personal responsibility. Under a socialist principle, including that of contemporary social democracy, the personal responsibility represented by the principle of liability is replaced by a principle of collective responsibility. Moreover, once it is recognized that there is no such thing as a collective will and that members of a collectivity differ in many ways, to speak of collective responsibility will be always to speak of some people pursuing their interests at the expense of others.[18]

The Capitalist Economy and the Moral Order

It is often claimed that capitalism may be good economically but is bad morally. This perceived disjunction between economics and ethics is used as justification for a mixed economy, where the task of policy is to develop a respectable tradeoff between economic and moral considerations.[19] A simple inspection of the moral order that underlies a capitalist economy or liberal democracy, however, renders suspect those common claims. A capitalist economy is simply an abstract noun that we use to describe the network of activities, conventions, and organizations that people develop when their relationships with one another are governed by the legal principles of property, contract, and liability.

That legal framework of a capitalist economy also involves a particular moral order, with both local and global dimensions. Locally, it constitutes a very concrete morality. A legal framework represented by the principles of property, contract, and tort involves moral content of a very concrete, personally manageable form. A legal principle of property can be stated equivalently as a moral injunction not to take what's not yours. Contract can be expressed in moral terms as a requirement to keep your promises. Tort can be represented morally as an obligation to make good on the wrongs you inflect on others. The legal institutions of capitalism clearly involve strong moral content, and of a highly practical character as compared with such philosophically abstract and remote notions as acting as if you were choosing behind a veil of ignorance.

Globally, the ethical character of capitalism does not require people to do what is beyond their power to do. It does not, for instance, say that people should act to save the world, so to speak, for this is as much an impossibility as is true central planning. Rather, it says that if people conduct themselves in accordance with the legal and moral principles noted above, they will contribute to the well being of all. It is the capitalist system itself that transforms, in conjunction with densely connected networks of social relationships, the local pursuit of essentially republican virtues into a global recipe for the advancement of all. A number of movie critics blasted *Forrest Gump* because the main character did not get involved in demonstrations, riots, and other save-the-world types of activities. Gump stuck to what was possible and manageable, and he dealt responsibly and caringly with everyone he encountered. Should others have acted similarly, the entire society might have been reformed. This reformation would not have been an intended or planned outcome but would have been an unintended by-product of personal conduct in densely connected society.

When historian and philosopher Gertrude Himmelfarb writes of the de-moralization of society over the past century, she is really characterizing what might be called the moral economy of social democracy.[20] It is often said that we learn from one another and that law can serve as an instrument of instruction. But we should ask what it is that is being learned, and taught. It turns out that dramatically different instruction is given under liberal and social democracy. Under liberal democracy, government is subject to law but is not the source of law. The production of law takes place in polycentric fashion, as illustrated by the classic characterization of the common law.[21] This system teaches that people are responsible for their conditions, save to the extent that they can identify particular people who have abridged their rights. Dissatisfaction with one's condition calls for a legal remedy only to the extent that an individual can identify particular people who have violated his rights and who thus bear some responsibility for his condition.

By contrast, under social democracy, government is a source of law through legislation. Someone who is discontent with his situation is counseled not to change his conduct but to lobby for favorable legislation. The source of discontent is held to reside not in inapt personal conduct but in some type of social deformity, correction of which requires legislation. For instance, abusers of alcohol and drugs may harm themselves in a system of liberal democracy, but have no reasonable basis for claiming that their condition has arisen because other people have violated their rights. Remedy requires the eradication of abuse, which is largely a matter of moral choice. Under a system of social democracy, however, there are strong interests operating to label such moral failing as diseases. This generates business for the providers of state-sponsored therapeutic services. It likewise provides support for the abusers, who are thereby relieved of the responsibility for their condition. Both the abusers and the providers of state services can gain by declaring such abuse to qualify for disability payments under Supplemental Security Income (SSI). It has long been recognized that the economy of the commons is bad. What we might call the moral economy of the commons is surely no better.

Notes

[1]John Maynard Keynes, *Essays in Biography* (New York: W.W. Norton, 1951), 301. See also the discussion of Jevons in T. W. Hutchison, *A Review of Economic Doctrine, 1870–1929* (Oxford: Oxford University Press, 1953), 46–49.

[2]Henry George, *Progress and Poverty* [1879] (New York: Robert Shalkenbach Foundation, 1937).

[3]A fine source on this is Charles Murray, *Losing Ground: American Social Policy 1950–1980* (New York: Basic Books, 1984).

[4]Francis Fukuyama, *The End of History and the Last Man* (New York: Free Press, 1992).

[5]To be sure, Fukuyama identifies social democracy as simply one instance or manifestation of economic liberalism (e.g., p. 44). For a thoughtful treatment of the forces tending to transform a liberal democracy into a social democracy, see Anthony de Jasay, *The State* (Oxford: Basil Blackwell, 1985).

[6]The classic economic references are Frank H. Knight, "Some Fallacies in the Interpretation of Social Cost," *Quarterly Journal of Economics* 38 (1924): 582–606; and H. Scott Gordon, "The Economic Theory of a Common-Property Resource: The Fishery," *Journal of Political Economy* 62 (April 1954): 124–42. See also Garrett Hardin and John Baden, eds., *Managing the Commons* (San Francisco: W. H. Freeman, 1977); and Elinor Ostrom, *Governing the Commons* (Cambridge: Cambridge University Press, 1990).

[7]See Charles H. McIlwain, *Constitutionalism: Ancient and Modern*, rev. ed (Ithaca, NY: Cornell University Press, 1947).

[8]For a lucid examination of Mises and Hayek in relation to the contemporary revival of interest in Austrian economics, see Karen I. Vaughn, *Austrian Economics in America: The Migration of a Tradition* (Cambridge: Cambridge University Press, 1994).

[9]The distinction between order and organization is a central theme in Friedrich A. Hayek, *Rules and Order* (Chicago: University of Chicago Press, 1973).

[10]This is illustrated by Paul Craig Roberts' contention that the Soviet Union was not a planned economy but rather was "a polycentric system with signals that are irrational from the standpoint of economic efficiency." Paul Craig Roberts, *Alienation and the Soviet Economy* (Albuquerque: University of New Mexico Press, 1971), 84.

[11]Robert E. McCormick and Robert D. Tollison, *Politicians, Legislation, and the Economy* (Boston: Martinus Nijhoff, 1981).

[12]For a sharp contrast between the common policy perspective and the alternative, constitutional perspective, see Dwight R. Lee and Richard B. McKenzie, *Regulating Government* (Lexington, MA: D.C. Heath, 1987).

[13]Gordon Tullock, "The Welfare Costs of Tariffs, Monopolies, and Theft," *Economic Inquiry* 5 (June 1967): 224–32.

[14]This theme is developed in Gordon Tullock, "The Rhetoric and Reality of Redistribution," *Southern Economic Journal* 47 (April 1981): 895–907.

[15]Richard E. Wagner, "Grazing the Federal Budgetary Commons: The Rational Politics of Budgetary Irresponsibility," *Journal of Law and Politics*, 9 (Fall 1992): 105–19.

[16]On corporate welfare, see Laurence H. Kallen, *Corporate Welfare* (New York: Carol Publishing Group, 1991); and Stephen Moore and Dean Stansel, "Ending Corporate Welfare as We Know It," Policy Analysis No.

225 (Washington: Cato Institute, 1995). More generally on the point that the impact of state policies on poverty cannot be assessed adequately by looking only at so-called anti-poverty programs, see Richard E. Wagner, *To Promote the General Welfare* (San Francisco, Pacific Research Institute, 1989).

[17]Walter Eucken, *Grundsatze der Wirtschaftspolitik* (Tubingen: J.C.B. Mohr, 1952). See also, Stephen C. Littlechild, *The Fallacy of the Mixed Economy* (London: Institute of Economic Affairs, 1978).

[18]This is one of the central themes of the recent scholarship on public choice, careful presentations of which can be found in such works as Hans van den Doel and Ven van Velthoven, *Democracy and Welfare Economics*, 2nd ed. (Cambridge: Cambridge University Press, 1992); and Dennis C. Mueller, *Public Choice II* (Cambridge: Cambridge University Press, 1989).

[19]See, for instance, Arthur M. Okun, *Equality and Efficiency: The Big Tradeoff* (Washington: Brookings Institution, 1975)

[20]Gertrude Himmelfarb, *The De-Moralization of Society: From Victorian Virtues to Modern Values* (New York: Alfred A. Knopf, 1995).

[21]See, for instance, Harold J. Berman, *Law and Revolution: The Formation of the Western Legal Tradition* (Cambridge: Harvard University Press, 1983); Arthur R. Hogue, *Origins of the Common Law* (Bloomington: Indiana University Press, 1966); and Bruno Leoni, *Freedom and the Law* (Los Angeles: Nash, 1960).

Gary Wolfram

Welfare Reform in Michigan

In January of 1991 I took a leave of absence from Hillsdale College in order to join Michigan Governor John Engler's administration as deputy state treasurer for taxation and economic policy. At the time, we were faced with a budget deficit of approximately $1.8 billion and a court case threatening $400 million of Single Business Tax revenues.

As the saying goes, every disaster is also an opportunity. The size of the budget problems allowed us to make more than marginal changes and to examine whether whole programs made sense. One program that made little policy sense and was a significant budget item was the welfare program known as "General Assistance." This was the state's welfare program for able-bodied persons who did not qualify for AFDC. For a number of years, state senate Republicans had recommended elimination of GA, but they had been thwarted by a Democratically controlled House and a Democratic governor.

In a bold move, Governor Engler pushed for elimination of General Assistance, which would save taxpayers some $250 million per year and eliminate some of the perverse and most destructive incentives of our welfare system. The Democratic Committee chairman at the time, Representative Hollister, agreed to let the bill out of committee for a floor vote. He believed that we would not be bold enough to garner the votes for the entire elimination of General Assistance. "The rest," as they say, "is history." The House passed the bill and the Governor signed it into law.

As might be expected when the Marxian view that "the history of all hitherto existing society is the history of class struggles" is the dominant basis for political debate, Governor Engler was attacked as "mean-spirited" for having the audacity to question the role of government in regard to welfare and to put his beliefs into action. How could he cut off taxpayer dollars to those who weren't working, while at the same time cutting taxes in order to revive a thoroughly stagnant state economy and provide job opportunities for those people?

The media heat was constant. I happened to be with the Governor when he was being interviewed by the British business journal, *The Economist*. I will always remember the question and response that concisely framed the Governor's position on welfare. The reporter asked: "Governor, what will you say to the media next winter when the first person who was thrown off General Assistance freezes to death on a Michigan street?"

Well, I was thinking, "That's a pretty good question. What are you going to say, John?"

The Governor's response was so quick that you knew it came from the heart as well as the head: "I'll ask where was that person's family?" Of course, that was the right answer. It was one of those points that seems so obvious that, when someone makes it, you wonder why you hadn't thought of it first.

Michigan's welfare system is based on two simple precepts: *responsibility* and *family*. People must be held responsible for their own actions. Austrian economist Friedrich A. Hayek put it best many years ago in *The Constitution of Liberty*:

> Liberty and responsibility are inseparable. A free society will not function or maintain itself unless its members regard it as right that each individual occupy the position that results from his action and accept it as due to his own action.[1]

The second precept is that the family structure is essential to a free and civilized society. The welfare system has driven families apart and created an incentive for many individuals to have children without a stable family structure. As Hillsdale College's Professor John Willson has written:

> We must trust that we will be given life and nurture. Every great and decent society that has ever existed has recognized this. Every brutal and disorderly society that has ever existed has put other things ahead of family. If you believe in the Hebrew and Christian Bibles, you know this deep in your heart, for there is nothing more deeply embedded in the Judeo-Christian heritage than the bonds of family life. Skeptics and unbelievers need merely to look around at experience and history. When families break up, societies disintegrate.[2]

In 1992, Michigan's welfare reform plan, called "To Strengthen Michigan Families," was begun. While the details are interesting, they can be summarized in the following:

(1) increasing efforts at training welfare recipients, both for employment and for self-employment;

(2) eliminating requirements for AFDC recipients that encourage family breakup, such as the 100-hour work limitation;

(3) reducing the tax rate on earned income;

(4) simplifying of benefits, such as cash instead of food stamps;

(5) allowing a buy-in of medical coverage;

(6) developing "Families First" program to hold together at-risk families;

(7) increasing collection of child support payments;

(8) signing of a social contract whereby welfare recipients agree to provide 20 hours or more each week to employment and/or education, including training, or community service.

Clearly, much of the effort is to prepare people to accept responsibility for their actions by educating and training them for the job market. Since a booming economy is the best remedy for poverty, we can also cite the Engler administration's success at reducing the state's tax burden, particularly for small and new businesses, as the best welfare reform package in the country. Raising the threshold for filing Single Business Tax forms from $40,000 in gross receipts to $250,000 in gross receipts, along with two other important and, indeed, unprecedented, victories—the elimination of the state's Inheritance Tax and the reduction of the state's property tax—have made it possible for thousands of new jobs and businesses to spring up.

The thrust of welfare reform in Michigan is to get welfare recipients to accept that they, not government, are responsible for their lives and that they must be able to produce something of value to the community in order to prosper. It attempts to reduce some of the egregious negative incentives of the current system, such as the effective taxation of earned income at rates of more than 100 percent, and it helps those who want to escape the vicious cycle of welfare dependency.

It also attempts to remove the impediments to family stability that the current welfare system breeds. It is well documented how the current system encourages fatherless families. Indeed, government attempts to substitute itself for the father. In Michigan, we are fighting against these disincentives. Rather than punishing a family for staying together and having one person work to support the rest, we encourage the family to stay together by eliminating provisions such as the 100-hour work limitation, and the 100 percent tax rate on earned income

Another thrust of Michigan's welfare reform has been to bring the community back into the system of support. The Michigan "Communities First" program, which allows some pilot communities to serve their own preferred mix of services, is an example. The administration has also relied on charitable organizations such as the Salvation Army and local churches to provide state-supported services or to provide charitable services in conjunction with state programs. This is an important part of the welfare reform, as it begins to bring together the person giving and the person receiving.

Since welfare became an entitlement program thirty years ago, the problems envisioned by the English philosopher Herbert Spencer some 150 years earlier have become apparent. In discussing the "poor laws" of mid-nineteenth century England, he wrote something worth quoting at length, for it gets to the heart of the moral principle involved in state welfare entitlements:

> Again, the moral effect of a poor law upon the rate-paying portion of the community is little considered, although it is one of its important features. Here also, there is an evident analogy between established religion and established charity. It is said, that in a system like that of our national church, in which the visible duties of a communicant, consist chiefly in attendance upon pubic worship, reception of the sacraments, payment of tithes, church rates, etc., the form will always be substituted for the reality; that the periodical ceremonies will take the place of the daily practice; that the physical will take place of the spiritual. It may be said, with equal truth, that a similar effect will follow the establishment of a poor law; the same principles are acted upon; the payment of poor rates will supplant the exercise of the moral duty. Forced contributions rarely appeal to the kindly feelings. The man who is called upon for a rate, does not put his hand into his pocket out of pure sympathy for the poor; he looks upon the demand as another tax, and feels annoyance rather than pleasure in paying it. Nor does the effect end here. The poor labourer or artisan, who is struggling hard with the world to maintain his independence, excites no pity. So long as there is a poor law, he cannot starve, and it will be time enough to consider his case when he applies for relief. The beggar

who knocks at his door, or the wayworn traveler who accosts him in his walk, is told to go to his parish; there is no need to inquire into his history, and to give him private assistance if found deserving, for there is already a public provision for him. Such is the state of mind encouraged by a national charity. When the legal demand is paid, the conscience is satisfied; the party is absolved from all exercise of generosity; charity is administered by proxy; the nobler feelings are never required to gain the victory over the selfish propensities; a dormant condition of those feelings necessarily follows, and depreciation of the national character is the final result. The payment of poor rates bears the same relation to real charity, that the attention to forms and ceremonies bears to real religion.[3]

This is what we find in Charles Dickens' famous story, *A Christmas Carol.* Recall that when the two people come in to collect money for the charity for the poor, Scrooge asks whether the state institutions for debtors were still in operation: "The treadmill and the poor law, are they in full vigour then?"[4] Today, most of us must admit that we have this same attitude. When we see a poor person on the street, do we stop and try to find out about that person, and do we ask how we might help them? Or do we think, "Boy, I send off forty percent of my income to government, so haven't I already paid enough to handle this kind of person? Let the welfare office take care of him."

Even worse, the current system has created a tension between those who are working and earning very little and those who are on welfare. When we are down at the local garage, we are likely to hear complaints from the shop mechanic about how the person ahead of him at the checkout line was using food stamps and also buying cigarettes and beer and potato chips. Not only do we not feel that it is not our job to assist those who are worse off, we feel that everyone who is on welfare is using the system to live off our sweat and toil.

By reforming welfare to help only those who cannot survive any other way, we will be once again freeing ourselves to provide true charity. Sometimes it is very hard to find a Good Samaritan in the 1990s, because all "wounded travelers" are supposed to be sent to the nearest office of the Department of Social Services. But in Michigan, the elimination of General Assistance immediately resulted in hundreds of churches getting together to provide shelter for the homeless on a rotating basis. When not shackled by government, the average citizen will also respond with heartfelt charity. Far from being "mean-spirited," Governor Engler's new welfare reform movement shows a strong belief in the natural goodness of mankind. His response, "Where was that person's family?" is really a broader question directed to all of us. Where were we? Where was our community? And by "community," I do not mean government.

We should not see welfare as a way of life for ourselves or for anyone in our community. Accepting this premise will help all of us lead better lives. And there is a special benefit for those of us who will never be on welfare. We will be challenged to look into our hearts and into the hearts of our fellow citizens and to respond to God that we, not government, are our brother's keeper.

Notes

[1]Friedrich A. Hayek, *The Constitution of Liberty* (Chicago: University of Chicago Press, 1960), 71.
[2]Quoted from personal correspondence, August 1990.
[3]Herbert Spencer, "The Proper Sphere of Government," in *The Man Versus the State* (Indianapolis: Liberty Classics, 1982), 198.
[4]Charles Dickens, *A Christmas Carol* [1852] (Brimax Books, 1992), 14.

Pete du Pont

The Conservative Vision and the Demise of the Welfare State

Any discussion of the demise of the welfare state must begin with some familiar words:

> We hold these truths to be self-evident, that all men are created equal, that they are endowed by their Creator with certain Unalienable Rights, that among these are Life, Liberty, and the pursuit of Happiness.

So wrote Thomas Jefferson in 1776. But liberty throughout history has been hard-won. The blood of millions has been shed in defense of a simple idea: man's superiority to the state. Sometimes it doesn't come to bloodshed or revolution. The threat posed by the state to man's freedom is not always so clear. Sometimes it comes gradually, offered in tempting packages put forward by well-meaning people who believe with all their hearts that they know better how to improve the lot of all. All that is necessary is that we provide them with certain powers and that we sacrifice only a few of our freedoms in order to provide a better and more equal world for all. A better world, of course, as viewed by *them*.

That world is called the welfare state.

The welfare state is much more than a set of entitlements and subsidies—and its impact reaches much farther than the disadvantaged underclass it is designed to help. For at its core, the welfare state emphasizes group responsibility over individual responsibility. After all, the purpose of bureaucracy is to make group instead of individual decisions. It also emphasizes decisions by elite groups, and it derides the importance of personal effort.

Collective Morality

The pre-eminence of a collective morality is evident in all of the welfare state's manifestations, from its welfare programs' bias against the family, to affirmative actions' group preferences, to the lax enforcement of punishment in the criminal justice system. This collective morality levies what I call "spiritual taxes" across the breadth of our society. Here are just a few examples:

- A welfare mother who clipped food coupons and saved from her benefits accumulated $3,000 in savings toward sending her child to college. Welfare officials demanded that she return of the money and face criminal prosecution.
- New York City's school policies require distribution of condoms to children, even if their parents have objected in writing.
- The Ninth U.S. Circuit Court of Appeals ruled that passing over higher scoring police promotion applicants in favor of lower scoring members of preferred gender or racial groups was permitted under the 1991 Civil Rights Act.
- A Wisconsin man convicted more than thirty times for indecent exposure was turned down for a job as a park attendant. He sued on the grounds that he had never exposed himself in a park, only in libraries and laundromats. Wisconsin employment officials agreed there was "probable cause" that the flasher was the victim of illegal job discrimination.

Three characteristics are shared by these affronts to Americans' sense of fairness, morality, right and wrong. First, they are all decisions of government, the institution to which we have delegated the responsibility for making sensible public policy decisions. Second, they are the result of three decades of welfare state programs that teach that group rights are more important than individual responsibility. Third, they each impose a spiritual tax on individuals. They discourage effort, thwart ambition, and sow the seeds of contempt for family, society, government, and the rule of law. In the end, they sap the moral strength of the nation. But there is something more dangerous going on here as well. The welfare state asserts that there are no absolute rights and wrongs, no standards for distinguishing good from bad. The absence of moral judgment implicit in all its processes is viewed as a desirable characteristic.

These examples also underscore the failure of the intellectual and moral foundations of the welfare state. It is worth a moment to consider each.

Redistribution of Wealth

The first intellectual leg of the four-legged stool supporting the welfare state is the idea that politicians in Washington can redistribute the wealth of the nation. The income tax, for example, is based as much on the deductions and loopholes you're entitled to as on the amount of income you have. We have a kind of redistribution of wealth by loophole. The IRS code—all 9,400 pages of it—is the most intrusive element of government into our lives. Its program of redistribution is directed by politicians in Washington.

Similarly, government benefits—scholarships, grants and programs—distribute money based upon politically favored groups. This week may it be urban groups, next month rural ones, perhaps racial groups or farmers. There are all kinds of examples—gas rationing, agricultural subsidies, race norming of tests, wage and price controls, and so on. All these concepts have failed, and the public has come to realize that the redistribution of wealth by politicians doesn't work very well.

Decision-Making by the "Experts"

The second leg is the idea that the important decisions in your life are better left to trained professionals—the "experts"—than to you and your family. After all, they supposedly know better than you do what's good for you. The education of your children is one example: The curriculum, extracurricular activities, and the schools your children go to are all decided by a professional—real bureaucrat—somewhere far away. I recently participated in a debate on school choice in which my opponent asked, "Does Governor du Pont really believe that a teenage mother is better able to choose the education for her child than a trained professional?" You bet Governor du Pont believes that. At least the mother knows the child's name, his or her skills and temperament. The fellow with the yellow highlighter pen somewhere in the basement of the Education Department knows nothing about her child.

As you can see, advocates of the welfare state don't confine their meddling to economic affairs. They think that the racial composition of classrooms and the work force and grades and test scores are better decided by a bureaucracy on racial grounds than by employers, schools or colleges operating on the basis of merit. Yet there is no proof that their way works, much less that it is fair and equitable. This idea of "life-by-professional decision-making" has failed. Affirmative action has cost the country $200 billion. In education, teacher salaries are up 25 percent in inflation-adjusted dollars in the last thirty years, class size is down 33 percent, the overall operating cost has grown by three times, and SAT scores are down almost 75 points.

The Obsolete Work Ethic

The third leg is the idea that the work ethic is obsolete and old-fashioned. If you don't believe this is true, just look at the welfare system itself. There are only two rules for getting welfare in America: First, you may not work and, second, you may not be married to anyone who does. Work is treated as if it were a bad thing, so the welfare system discourages it. Similarly, if you and your neighbor each are cab drivers, and one of you works forty hours a week and the other sixty hours, the one who works more will be penalized with a higher tax rate. That's certainly an anti-work statute.

Another of my favorite examples concerns a school district in Delaware which abolished grades so that, as the superintendent declared self-righteously, "All children can be successful, not just the lucky few who happen to get an 'A.'" Did you ever *happen* to get an A? I don't think so. I think you worked for it. The idea that we are going to degrade the value of work in the classroom by not giving out "A"s is symptomatic of the failure of the welfare statists' thinking.

Moral Relativism

The fourth intellectual leg of the welfare state is moral relativism—the idea that there are no rights or wrongs, just different choices among alternative lifestyles. We saw this idea spread in the 1950s and 1960s regarding the Soviet Union. Those "good communists" had just formulated a different way of organizing life. The fact that they killed tens of millions of people in the process was not particularly relevant; it was just one of the elements of the system.

On one occasion, former Secretary of Education Bill Bennett was teaching a class in San Francisco, and a young student made this comment: If Bennett was from the government, he was probably lying to them—smart kid! So, the student continued, how could anyone tell which country was really better?

Bennett's reply was that he should apply the "gate theory." If the gates of each country were open, which way would the people flow? With the fall of the Berlin Wall in 1989, we began to see the gates open in Eastern Europe and the Soviet Union. The flood began with 1,000, 2,000 then 10,000 people a day fleeing to the West. There can no longer be a question about which system is better (except in such enclaves as Harvard University and the U.S. State Department, where nostalgia for the heydays of communism is still strong).

Multiculturalism—the idea that all cultures are equal— is also an expression of relativism. But are they really the same? Was Iran under the Ayatollah a culture just as good as America's? Was the Soviet Union—where you could serve ten years in a labor camp just for attending church—the moral equivalent of any Western democracy? Or what about ancient cultures? Were the Incas—who ripped the hearts out of young girls to sacrifice to the gods—a just and humane people? In some parts of the United States there are laws mandating that public schools must teach children to "understand that no culture is inherently superior to any other." (That is the exact wording of Florida's statute.) So are we to teach that the Nazi culture of the 1930s and 1940s was no better or worse than our own?

Moral relativism also champions "alternative families." After all, the relativists say, it is just a lifestyle choice to be married or unmarried or homosexual or heterosexual. Whether you have two parents or one, whether the parents are of the same sex, really doesn't make any difference. But this is plain nonsense, as our 2,000-year-old Judeo-Christian tradition and all the recent data on the break up of two-parent families, illegitimacy, violence, crime, poverty, and abuse show.

An Alternative to the Welfare State

The four cardinal principles of the welfare state have failed and the November 1994 election demonstrated that they have been overwhelmingly rejected by the American people. So what are we to do? Clearly, reforming the welfare state is not enough. Conservatives must offer a vision that is not just the opposite of the liberals' vision—advocating small government where the liberals favor big government, individualism where they favor group entitlements, free markets where they favor regulation. They must engage in a profound and fundamental "revisioning" of the entire philosophy of American government.

Let me suggest the core principles of that vision.

A Common Culture

First, there is an American culture, a set of common and widely shared beliefs, that binds our society together and defines the behavior expected of its members. Our common language is the most obvious element. More profound elements are our religious heritage, the two-parent family as the foundation of society, the concept of merit, and the work ethic. That is not to say there are no Americans who profess atheism, speak other languages, or choose not to have families. But to be a part of America's culture, one accepts that the state will not be neutral regarding every set of ideas and that certain values, customs, and beliefs will be cherished and reinforced by the institutions of our society.

Thus, governmental action attacking the role of religion in our lives, undermining the authority of parents or embracing multiculturalism has no place. What does have a place is requiring public schools to teach in English, allowing invocations before graduation, and encouraging schools to grade on merit. We must reward the pursuit of excellence, too, for both brain surgeons and bricklayers must be committed to excellence if we are to prosper. Adjustment of test scores or standards to equalize results among societal groups undermines effort, merit and equality of opportunity.

Equality of Opportunity

Second, there must be no subsets of American citizens. We need to reaffirm the Fourteenth Amendment's equal protection clause and erase from our laws group-rights statutes. Legal preferences based upon race or gender existing in law should be repealed. This movement toward ending preferences as well as discrimination based on race, sex, origin, or creed has already begun in states like California. It is the beginning of the restoration of liberty and individualism in American social policy.

Eventually, even the federal government must abandon the utopian concept of equality of results. Policies designed to guarantee results quickly produce the lowest common denominator while costing individuals their liberty, the opportunity to excel, and the benefits of success. We must emphasize instead the crucial importance of individual opportunity and economic growth. For as philosopher Michael Novak has noted, "Real differences in talent, aspiration, and application inexorably individuate humans...no fair and free system can possibly guarantee equal outcomes. A democratic system depends for its legitimacy, therefore, not upon equal results but upon a sense of equal opportunity."

Economic Freedom

Third, we must return to a market economy—history's only mechanism through which ordinary citizens can benefit from rising living standards. It is our nation's first economic priority. To accelerate economic growth, we should repeal the Bush and Clinton tax increases. Then we should enact a flat tax to abolish all loopholes and tax shelters. Prosperity also requires open markets—the right to choose among foreign and domestic products. Protectionism is a statist policy that retards economic growth, reduces the choices and raises the prices we pay for goods. Passage of the GATT Agreement was a first step in the right direction.

Federalism

Fourth, both common sense and our Constitution demand a return to the principles of federalism. Limiting federal spending to less than 20 percent of GNP will begin to shrink the national government and direct more responsibility and opportunity to individuals as well as state and local governments. In this context, we must assert unambiguously the proposition that government exists to promote freedom. Individuals must be able to choose the health care appropriate to their families, not be required to enter some tangle of regulations negotiated in a distant bureaucracy which doesn't know their names, let alone their needs. People must also be free to choose the schools— public or private—most suitable for their children.

Work, Not Welfare

Finally, low income families deserve freedom, too. The replacement of the work ethic by the welfare state has destroyed the opportunity, the dignity, and the cohesion of poor families in America. The individual responsibility of doing a good job, earning a living, and striving for improvement is crucial to restoring opportunity and self-respect to Americans trapped in the "underclass." It is time to replace welfare with work.

The spiritual taxes of the welfare state directly attack the poor and rich alike, communicating to society that government values—collective values—take precedence over individual initiative and responsibility. These taxes are indeed the root cause of the current decline in the quality of life in America amidst abundant prosperity.

Welfare statism and the corrosive values it teaches are democracy's version of state tyranny. Our task is to overthrow this tyranny and replace it with a philosophy of personal freedom, moral responsibility and individual opportunity, which will inevitably provide a more bountiful, rewarding, just, and equal society.

If common men, ennobled by the divine spark of their Creator, are, in Winston Churchill's phrase, to "move forward into broad, sunlit uplands," they must do so one by one, striving to advance their individual progress toward that uplifting goal. There are no collective means to either morality or individual prosperity.

Gleaves Whitney

Life After Welfare

The remarkable thing about the welfare debate today is that virtually no one is defending the status quo. There has been a sea change in the public's perception of the problem. The Berlin Wall around the welfare state is falling. And it is falling because, after decades of trying to wage a "war on poverty," the verdict is in: The Great Society was a great mistake.

The old model of Washington, D.C.'s "War on Poverty" was one of the most grandiose projects in human history. It led to the transfer of some $5 trillion to the poor and created hundreds of programs. But what does our nation have to show for this "domestic Vietnam"? We cannot even say that it has been a stalemate. Tragically, the Great Society helped stall what had been a twenty-year decline in the poverty rate, and it actually worsened the plight of the poor by rewarding "behavior poverty" with a slew of perverse incentives. By any standard, America has lost this war.

Imagine if every evening, our TV news anchors added up the body count of the casualties caused by the War on Poverty—think of the number of families that have been broken up, and the number of young people who have dropped out. Do you think the public would have the will to continue pursuing the same strategy year after year? After all, the body count in this war is not 5,000 miles away. It can be tallied down on Main Street.

A New Approach to Welfare Reform: Devolution

How do we deconstruct a system that breaks up families, discourages work, and destroys lives? Michigan Governor John Engler has been taking the national lead in arguing that a totally new approach is needed. He argues that radical reform can only take place if there is a fundamental change in the relationship between the federal government and the states. It is time to reverse the course of a mighty river of power that, for the last sixty years, has been flowing in the wrong direction—toward Washington, D.C. It is time to set that river back on the course the Founders of this nation intended—and send more power to the states.

"Devolution" is what it is called these days. We keep telling the media in Lansing and in Washington, D.C.: "There is no 'devil' in devolution." But liberals harp on devolution as though it were a satanic rite rather than the rightful return of power to the people at the state and local level. In Congress and the Clinton administration, liberals are resisting devolution and playing politics with welfare reform. To them, the poor are a voting block to be bribed with the coinage of class warfare, and the dollars of the middle class.

It is too early to tell whether the conservative seeds being sown in Congress will actually take root and grow to maturity. Some are suggesting that the Senate will be the graveyard for much of the Contract with America. But there are good signs nevertheless. In Williamsburg after last November's elections, for example, an extraordinary thing happened: Newt Gingrich approached Governor Engler and asked him and other Republican governors to write the welfare bills that Congress should consider. So the governors accepted the offer and several have since become lead architects in demolishing the current system of federal entitlements, and replacing it with block grants to the fifty states.

Deregulation

Important as the congressional theater is, we must be mindful of the bigger picture. There are many ways Washington, D.C. imposes its power on the rest of us, and not just through the laws and mandates passed by Congress. When Lady Thatcher was at Hillsdale College in 1994, she uttered one of those unforgettable lines she's known for: "Government is taking too much from us to do too much to us."

In Washington D.C., the two branches of government that will continue to threaten our freedom—in a roundabout and therefore more dangerous manner—are the judicial and executive branches. They have amassed a frightening degree of regulatory power. In fact, much of the real power in America today is in the hands of judges and bureaucrats. So much so that it's fair to say that our country is ruled by twin tyrants—on the one hand, by a judicial oligarchy intent on micromanaging our lives from the bench, and on the other, by the numerous alphabetical departments—HUD, HHS, DOT, DOE—most of which we wish were DOA.

I can imagine a scenario in which Congress gives up much of its power and returns it to the states, only to have bureaucrats try to impose their will through new rules and regulations. The thing about bureaucrats is that they don't ever give up. You can seek waivers and try to beat them in court, but you know what they do? They gin up more rules for the rest of us to follow in order to make their existence necessary.

Remember reading a few years ago about that renegade Japanese soldier found on a remote island of Indonesia who was still fighting World War II? He was still hanging on forty-five years later, living in a cave, waving a machete. Finally, social workers were called in to plant Japanese flags all around his cave and shout at him through loud speakers that the war was over. He could go home now. Still, he refused to surrender. That same stubbornness exists in the federal bureaucracy. That man in the caves, still fighting the war—he's the bureaucrats' patron saint.

Now, if the leftover liberals in Congress insist that the federal bureaucrats know best, Governor Engler has a proposal to make: Let those bureaucrats run the District of Columbia. They can have it. Let the congressional committee supervising D.C. serve as the city council. Put its members to the test and find out how good they are. See if street crime goes down. See if illegitimacy goes down. See if schools become safer and education performance goes up. If Donna Shalala and the bureaucrats at the Department of Health and Human Services think they can manage welfare better than the states, give HHS the District of Columbia on which to experiment. Let the District of Columbia be a nationally run experiment in unrestricted, full-blown welfare statism and compare its performance with the fifty states. Governor Engler is not ordinarily a betting man, but he is pretty sure he knows who's going to lose that wager.

Letting the States Experiment

The Governor has been pushing hard for all three branches of the national government to back off and bug out when it comes to welfare. Let Michigan and the other states fix, or better yet, replace, a broken system. In a three-month period in early 1995, the Governor made nine trips to Washington, D.C. to meet with the leadership in Congress. He lobbied them to collapse over 330 programs into eight block grants, so that states could have the flexibility to implement the solutions that work best for them.

Under the block grant approach, there will be more accountability at the state level than at the federal level. Furthermore, here in Michigan, we guarantee that our Department of Social Services will shrink in size if Washington gives up its money and power. It will shrink, first of all, because it won't labor under a mountain of federal laws, and second because it can contract out many of its services.

But conservatives in Washington are split over Governor Engler's proposal to devolve the welfare system. On the one hand, one group, led by the Cato Institute, is supportive of getting the national government out of the poverty industry. The members of this group are impressed by what this Governor and others have done in the past two years—in Wisconsin, New Jersey, and New Hampshire—to deconstruct the Great Society. On the other hand, there is another group, led by the Heritage Foundation, which is skeptical of the states' ability to make any real dent in the welfare problem. Their reigning analyst, Robert Rector, is calling for conservative micromanagement from inside the Beltway.

Governor Engler agrees with the first group and rejects Rector's remedy. Conservative micromanagement is hardly any better than liberal micromanagement. Bureaucrats in Washington are too far distant to see the problem in its full moral, psychological, and social dimensions. To whom are they answerable? That argument, of course, is not original with us. It was the great insight of Austrian economists Ludwig von Mises and Friedrich A. Hayek, who understood that knowledge is radically decentralized and that big statist solutions do not work.

Liberals attack Governor Engler's proposals on entirely different grounds. Because of the civil-rights battles of the 1950s and 1960s, they are skeptical that devolution will lead to a just treatment of the poor. They are looking for any hint of mean-spiritedness in the debate, and they are suspicious that some states would throw young mothers out on the streets and allow children to starve. This, of course, is absurd. In the first place, there is not a governor or state legislature in America that wants young women and their children to go naked and hungry on our streets. Second, it is a curious argument that the national government in Washington, D.C. is more concerned about the needy than state governments in Lansing, Austin, or Albany, which are so much closer to the problem. Third, competition among the states will provide a powerful incentive to get welfare reform right. Governors and legislators will be held accountable by voters. Elected officials will rise or fall based on their ability to put incentives in place that are not socially destructive. Politicians will be looking across state lines at who is doing the best job reforming the system, turning lives around, and saving taxpayer money. Indeed, the fifty states vying with one another will create what amounts to competitive market forces that cannot exist in the centralized bureaucracy we have today.

For argument's sake, say you do have a rogue, malevolent state legislature that wants to punish women and children. That state's so-called reforms are frankly going to fail, but the difference is this: It won't take thirty years to change. The nation would be better off taking the risk that one or two states might fail than sticking with the current system—which guarantees that all fifty states fail year after year after year.

Creating New Incentives

Based on Michigan's experience, we think state-based reform has a great chance to succeed—not just in saving dollars, but in turning lives around. And that is the real point. The conservative agenda is not to punish poor women and children, but to give them the strongest possible incentives to choose wisely. It is hard to blame the victims caught in the perverse snares of the current system. They are, in many cases, simply adapting to the rules government has devised and, in that light, are making rational choices. To give you some idea of just how perverse Washington's incentives have become, let me tell you about a case here in Michigan.

There is an AFDC client who lives in public housing. This person refuses to take part in our mandatory work program, so we sanctioned her by cutting her AFDC grant, which reduced her income. What was the result? Did she go to work? On the contrary, because of federal rules, when her income went down, her Section 8 public housing subsidy went up, and her Food Stamp allowance went up. That meant the initial sanction for not working was canceled out. She found herself better off at home, saying, in effect, "Make my day: Hit me with another 'sanction.'" From the taxpayers' point of view, her course of action was less than ideal. But, in its own way, her choice was rational—because the system made it rational.

If government is going to have anything to do with welfare, it needs to create incentives that encourage personal responsibility. Look at how, here in Michigan back in 1991, General Assistance caseloads dropped dramatically after the Governor said he would terminate the program subsidizing 80,000 able-bodied adults without children. The program wasn't going to end for nine months, but as soon as they heard, people started looking for alternatives, i.e., jobs. Similarly, look at New Jersey, which said it would no longer increase payments to welfare mothers who have additional children. Since then, the birth-rate among those mothers has dropped about 15 percent.

State government has a critically important role to play in welfare reform. First, it should take a kind of Hippocratic oath to "do no harm to the poor." Then it should put incentives in place that encourage responsible behavior. Let me illustrate with another Michigan example. One of the things Governor Engler insisted on, from the beginning, is that aid be a two-way street: You don't get something for nothing. After all, work is the reality for most Americans. It is not fair that some welfare recipients can sit at home better off than their neighbors who are hard at work just trying to make ends meet. That is why, early in his first term, he reformed Aid to Families with Dependent Children by requiring recipients to sign a "Social Contract" that committed them either to work, job training, or volunteer service for at least 20 hours a week.

Because of our Social Contract and related reforms, Michigan now has one of the strongest welfare-to-work track records in the nation. Some 55,000 cases have been closed because recipients got a job and are now self-reliant. And we have saved our state and the federal government over $100 million in the first two years. We are not satisfied; we want the numbers to be higher. But we are off to a good start—because people are working and their work is paying.

A Moral Devolution

Up to this point, I have commented only about Washington, D.C. giving money and power back to the states. But Governor Engler knows that political devolution is only a halfway house to meeting the welfare challenge. That is because welfare is not just a political problem. It is a moral problem. There is a limit to what state government can do. If twentieth-century history teaches us anything, it is that central planning does not work. Only individual planning does. Thoughtful conservatives have understood all along that big government cannot wage a War on Poverty from inside the Beltway or from inside a state and expect to win it.

Under the old system that author Marvin Olasky so eloquently describes in his book *The Tragedy of American Compassion* —when there was welfare but not a "welfare state"—a needy person went to family members, to the church, or to a local relief organization and asked for assistance. There was personal contact—and there were personal consequences. Over the decades, the whole process has become more and more centralized and less and less personalized. Distant lawmakers and bureaucrats now determine who is "entitled" to welfare. It is a *fait accompli* with no reciprocal obligations on the part of the needy. The social stigma has given way to the social service.

In any case, we need first to free the power and money that

have been held captive in Washington, D.C.—not to hoard them in our state capitols or city halls—but ultimately to return authority and responsibility to where they belong—to civil society—to our families and neighborhoods, churches and charitable organizations. These institutions are on the front lines of poverty. The volunteers working in these institutions understand its causes and consequences. Only when civil society is more actively engaged in the debate will we succeed in truly reforming the system. That is the time when more of our citizens will fare well in life rather than live life on welfare.

Ludwig von Mises

Reading 1: Poverty*

In this excerpt from Mises' monumental study, Human Action, *he demonstrates that the market economy has been the great eliminator of poverty. He also shows that often charity—with the best of intentions— has negative effects on the recipients.*

When in the ages preceding the rise of modern capitalism statesmen, philosophers, and lawyers referred to the poor and to the problems of poverty, they meant these supernumerary wretches. Laissez faire and its off-shoot, industrialism, converted the employable poor into wage earners. In the unhampered market society there are people with higher and people with lower incomes. There are no longer men, who, although able and ready to work, cannot find regular jobs because there is no room left for them in the social system of production. But liberalism and capitalism were even in their heyday limited to comparatively small areas of Western and Central Europe, North America, and Australia. In the rest of the world hundreds of millions still vegetate on the verge of starvation. They are poor or paupers in the old sense of the term, supernumerary and superfluous, a burden to themselves and a latent threat to the minority of their more lucky fellow citizens.

The penury of these miserable masses of—in the main col-

*From Ludwig von Mises, "The Welfare Principle vs. the Market Principle," *Human Action* [1949] (Chicago: Henry Regnery, 3rd rev. ed., 1966), 835–840.

ored—people is not caused by capitalism, but by the absence of capitalism. But for the triumph of laissez faire, the lot of the peoples of Western Europe would have been even worse than that of the coolies. What is wrong with Asia is that the per capita quota of capital invested is extremely low when compared with the capital equipment of the West. The prevailing ideology and the social system which is its off-shoot check the evolution of profit-seeking entrepreneurship. There is very little domestic capital accumulation, and manifest hostility to foreign investors. In many of these countries the increase in population figures even outruns the increase in capital available.

It is false to blame the European powers for the poverty of the masses in their former colonial empires. In investing capital the foreign rulers did all they could do for an improvement in material well-being. It is not the fault of the whites that the oriental peoples are reluctant to abandon their traditional tenets and abhor capitalism as an alien ideology.

As far as there is unhampered capitalism, there is no longer any question of poverty in the sense in which this term is applied to the conditions of a noncapitalistic society. The increase in population figures does not create supernumerary mouths but additional hands whose employment produces additional wealth. There are no able-bodied paupers. Seen from the point of view of the economically backward nations, the conflicts between "capital" and "labor" in the capitalist countries appear as conflicts within a privileged upper class. In the eyes of the Asiatics, the American automobile worker is an "aristocrat." He is a man who belongs to the 2 percent of the earth's population whose income is highest. Not only the colored races but also the Slavs, the Arabs, and some other peoples look upon the average income of the citizens of the capitalistic countries—about 12 or 15 percent of the total of mankind—as a curtailment of their own material well-being. They fail to realize that the prosperity of these allegedly privileged groups is, apart from the effects of migration barriers, not paid for by their own poverty, and that the main obstacle to the improvement of their own conditions is their abhorrence of capitalism.

Within the frame of capitalism the notion of poverty refers only to those people who are unable to take care of themselves. Even if we disregard the case of children, we must realize that there will always be such unemployables. Capitalism, in improving the masses' standard of living, hygienic conditions, and methods of prophylactics and therapeutics, does not remove bodily incapacity. It is true that today many people who in the past would have been doomed to life-long disability are restored to full vigor. But, on the other hand, many whom innate defects, sickness or accidents would have extinguished sooner in earlier days, survive as permanently incapacitated people. Moreover, the prolongation of the average length of life tends toward an increase in the number of the aged who are no longer able to earn a living.

The problem of the incapacitated is a specific problem of human civilization and of society. Disabled animals must perish quickly. They either die of starvation or fall prey to the foes of their species. Savage man had no pity on those who were substandard. With regard to them many tribes practiced those barbaric methods of ruthless extirpation to which the Nazis resorted in our time. The very existence of a comparatively great number of invalids is, however paradoxical, a characteristic mark of civilization and material well-being.

Provision for those invalids who lack means of sustenance and are not taken care of by their next of kin has long been considered a work of charity. The funds needed have sometimes been provided by governments, more often by voluntary contributions. The Catholic orders and congregations and some Protestant institutions have accomplished marvels in collecting such contributions and in using them properly. Today there are also many nondenominational establishments vying with them in noble rivalry.

The charity system is criticized for two defects. One is the paucity of the means available. However, the more capitalism progresses and increases wealth, the more sufficient become the charity funds. On the one hand, people are more ready to donate in proportion to the improvement in their own well-being. On the other hand, the number of the needy drops concomitantly. Even for those with moderate incomes the opportunity is offered, by savings and insurance policies, to provide for accidents, sickness, old age, the education of their children, and the support of widows and orphans. It is highly probable that the funds of the charitable institutions would be sufficient in the capitalist countries if interventionism were not to sabotage the essential institutions of the market economy. Credit expansion and inflationary increase of the quantity of money frustrate the "common man's" attempts to save and to accumulate reserves for less propitious days. But the other procedures of interventionism are hardly less injurious to the vital interests of the wage earners and salaried employees, the professions, and the owners of small-size business. The greater part of those assisted by charitable institutions are needy only because interventionism has made them so. At the same time inflation and the endeavors to lower the rate of interest below the potential market rates virtually expropriate the endowments of hospitals, asylums, orphanages, and similar establishments. As far as the welfare propagandists lament the insufficiency of the funds available for assistance, they lament one of the results of the policies that they themselves are advocating.

The second defect charged to the charity system is that it is charity and compassion only. The indigent has no legal claim to the kindness shown to him. He depends on the mercy of benevolent people, on the feelings of tenderness which his distress arouses. What he receives is a voluntary gift for which he must be grateful. To be an almsman is shameful and humiliating. It is an unbearable condition for a self-respecting man.

These complaints are justified. Such shortcomings do indeed inhere in all kinds of charity. It is a system that corrupts both givers and receivers. It makes the former self-righteous and the latter submissive and cringing. However, it is only the mentality of a capitalistic environment that makes people feel the indignity of giving and receiving alms. Outside of the field of the cash nexus and of deals transacted between buyers and sellers in a purely businesslike manner, all interhuman relations are tainted by the same failing. It is precisely the absence of this personal element in market transactions that all those deplore who blame capitalism for hard-heartedness and callousness. In the eyes of such critics cooperation under the *do ut des* principle dehumanizes all societal bonds. It substitutes contracts for brotherly love and readiness to help one another. These critics indict the legal order of capitalism for its neglect of the "human side." They are inconsistent when they blame the charity system for its reliance upon feelings of mercy.

Feudal society was founded on acts of grace and on the gratitude of those favored. The mighty overlord bestowed a benefit upon the vassal, and the latter owed him personal fidelity. Conditions were human in so far as the subordinates had to kiss their superiors' hands and to show allegiance to them. In a feudal environment the element of grace inherent in charitable acts did not give offense. It agreed with the generally accepted ideology and practice. It is only in the setting of a society based entirely upon contractual bonds that the idea emerged of giving to the indigent a legal claim, an actionable title to sustenance against society.

The metaphysical arguments advanced in favor of such a right to sustenance are based on the doctrine of natural right. Before God or nature all men are equal and endowed with an inalienable right to live. However, the reference to inborn equality is certainly out of place in dealing with the effects of inborn inequality. It is a sad fact that physical disability prevents many people from playing an active role in social cooperation. It is the operation of the laws of nature that makes these people outcasts. They are stepchildren of God or nature. We may fully endorse the religious and ethical precepts that declare it to be man's duty to assist his unlucky brethren whom nature has doomed. But the recognition of this duty does not answer the question concerning what methods should be resorted to for its performance. It does not enjoin the choice of methods which would endanger society and curtail the productivity of human effort. Neither the able-bodied nor the incapacitated would derive any benefit from a drop in the quantity of goods available.

The problems involved are not of a praxeological character, and economics is not called upon to provide the best possible solution for them. They concern pathology and psychology. They refer to the biological fact that the fear of penury and of the degrading consequences of being supported by charity are important factors in the preservation of man's physiological equilibrium. They impel a man to keep fit, to avoid sickness and accidents, and to recover as soon as possible from injuries suffered. The experience of the social security system, especially that of the oldest and most complete scheme, the German, has clearly shown the undesirable effects resulting from the elimination of these incentives.[1] No civilized community has callously allowed the incapacitated to perish. But the substitution of a legally enforceable claim to support or sustenance for charitable relief does not seem to agree with human nature as it is. Not metaphysical prepossessions, but considerations of practical expediency make it inadvisable to promulgate an actionable right to sustenance.

It is, moreover, an illusion to believe that the enactment of such laws could free the indigent from the degrading features inherent in receiving alms. The more openhanded these laws are, the more punctilious must their application become. The discretion of bureaucrats is substituted for the discretion of people whom an inner voice drives to acts of charity. Whether this change renders the lot of those incapacitated any easier, is hard to say.

Notes

[1]Sulzbach, *German Experience with Social Insurance* (New York, 1947), 22–32.

Ludwig von Mises

Reading 2: Compulsory Social Insurance and Unemployment Insurance*

In another important, pioneering work, Socialism, *Ludwig von Mises explains the negative and perverse effects of state-provided health care and unemployment insurance. The solution to these social problems is to free the market from government intervention.*

Compulsory Social Insurance

The essence of the programme of German statism is social insurance. But people outside the German Empire have also come to look upon social insurance as the highest point to which the insight of the statesman and political wisdom can attain. If some praise the wonderful results of these institutions, others can only reproach them for not going far enough, for not including all classes and for not giving the favored all that, in their opinion, they should have. Social insurance, it was said, ultimately aimed at giving every citizen adequate care and the best medical treatment in sickness and adequate sustenance if he should become incapable of work through accident, sickness or old age, or if he should fail to find work on conditions he considered necessary.

---

*From Ludwig von Mises, "Methods of Destructionism," *Socialism,* rev. ed. [1951] (Indianapolis: Liberty Classics, 1981), 475–478 and 484–487.

No ordered community has callously allowed the poor and incapacitated to starve. There has always been some sort of institution designed to save from destitution people unable to sustain themselves. As general well-being has increased hand in hand with the development of capitalism, so too has the relief of the poor improved. Simultaneously the legal basis of this relief has changed. What was formerly a charity on which the poor had no claim is now a duty of the community. Arrangements are made to ensure the support of the poor. But at first people took care not to give the individual poor a legally enforceable claim to support or sustenance. In the same way they did not at once think of removing the slight stigma attaching to all who were thus maintained by the community. This was not callousness. The discussions which grew out of the English Poor Laws in particular show that people were fully conscious of the great social dangers involved in every extension of poor relief.

German social insurance and the corresponding institutions of other states are constructed on a very different basis. Maintenance is a claim which the person entitled to it can enforce at law. The claimant suffers no slur on his social standing. He is a state pensioner like the king or his ministers or the receiver of an insurance annuity, like anyone else who has entered into an insurance contract. There is also no doubt that he is entitled to look on what he receives as the equivalent of his own contributions. For the insurance contributions are always at the expense of wages, immaterial of whether they are collected from the entrepreneur or from the workers. What the entrepreneur has to pay for the insurance is a charge on labor's marginal productivity; it thus tends to reduce the wages of labor. When the costs of maintenance are provided out of taxes the worker clearly contributes towards them, directly or indirectly.

To the intellectual champions of social insurance, and to the politicians and statesmen who enacted it, illness and health appeared as two conditions of the human body sharply separated from each other and always recognizable without difficulty or doubt. Any doctor could diagnose the characteristics of "health." "Illness" was a bodily phenomenon which showed itself independently of human will, and was not susceptible to influence by will. There were people who for some reason or other simulated illness, but a doctor could expose the pretense. Only the healthy person was fully efficient. The efficiency of the sick person was lowered according to the gravity and nature of his illness, and the doctor was able, by means of objectively ascertainable physiological tests, to indicate the degree of the reduction of efficiency in percentages of normal efficiency.

Now every statement in this theory is false. There is no clearly defined frontier between health and illness. Being ill is not a phenomenon independent of conscious will and of psychic forces working in the subconscious. A man's efficiency is not merely the result of his physical condition; it depends largely on his mind and will. Thus the whole idea of being able to separate, by medical examination, the unfit from the fit and from the malingerers, and those able to work from those unable to work, proves to be untenable. Those who believed that accident and health insurance could be based on completely effective means of ascertaining illnesses and injuries and their consequences were very much mistaken. The destructionist aspect of accident and health insurance lies above all in the fact that such institutions promote accidents and illness, hinder recovery, and very often create or at any rate intensify and lengthen, the functional disorders which follow illness or accident.

A special disease, traumatic neurosis, which had already appeared in some cases as a result of the legal regulation of claims for compensation for injury, has been thus turned into a national disease by compulsory social insurance. No one any longer denies that traumatic neurosis is a result of social legislation. Overwhelming statistics show that insured persons take much longer time to recover from their injuries than other persons, and that they are liable to more extensions and permanent functional disturbances than those of the uninsured. Insurance against diseases breeds disease. Individual observation by doctors as well as statistics prove that recovery from illnesses and injuries is much slower in officials and permanent employees and people compulsorily insured than in members of the professions and those not insured. The desire and the necessity of becoming well again and ready for work as soon as possible assist recuperation to a degree so great as to be capable of demonstration.[1]

To feel healthy is quite different from being healthy in the medical sense, and a man's ability to work is largely independent of the physiologically ascertainable and measurable performances of his individual organs. The man who does not want to be healthy is not merely a malingerer. He is a sick person. If the will to be well and efficient is weakened, illness and inability to work is caused. By weakening or completely destroying the will to be well and able to work, social insurance creates illness and inability to work; it produces the habit of complaining—which is in itself a neurosis—and neuroses of other kinds. In short, it is an institution which tends to encourage disease, not to say accidents, and to intensify considerably the physical and psychic results of accidents and illnesses. As a social institution it makes a people sick bodily and mentally or at least helps to multiply, lengthen, and intensify disease.

The psychic forces which are active in every living thing, including man, in the form of a will to health and a desire to work, are not independent of social surroundings. Certain circumstances strengthen them, others weaken them. The social environment of an African tribe living by hunting is decidedly calculated to stimulate these forces. The same is true of the quite different environment of the citizens of a capitalist society, based on division of labor and on private property. On the other hand, a social order weakens these forces when it promises that if the individual's work is hindered by illness or the effects of a trauma he shall live without work or with little work and suffer no very noticeable reduction in his income.

Matters are not so simple as they appear to the naive pathology of the army or prison doctor.

Social insurance has thus made the neurosis of the insured a dangerous public disease. Should the institution be extended and developed the disease will spread. No reform can be of any assistance. We cannot weaken or destroy the will to health without producing illness.

Unemployment Insurance

Assistance of the unemployed has proved to be one of the most effective weapons of destructionism.

The reasoning which brought about unemployment insurance was the same as that which led to the setting up of insurance against sickness and accident. Unemployment was held to be a misfortune which overwhelmed men like an avalanche. It occurred to no one that lack of wages would be a better term than lack of employment, for what the unemployed person misses is not work but the remuneration of work. The point was not that the "unemployed" could not find work, but that they were not willing to work at the wages they could get in the labor market for the particular work they were able and willing to perform.

The value of health and accident insurance becomes problematic by reason of the possibility that the insured person may himself bring about, or at least intensify, the condition insured against. But in the case of unemployment insurance, the condition insured against can never develop unless the insured persons so will. If they did not act as trade unionists, but reduced their demands and changed their locations and occupations according to the requirements of the labor market, they could eventually find work. For as long as we live in the real world and not in the Land of Heart's Desire, labor will be a scarce good, that is, there will be an unsatisfied demand for labor. Unemployment is a problem of wages, not of work. It is just as impossible to insure against unemployment as it would be to insure against, say, the unsaleability of commodities.

Unemployment insurance is definitely a misnomer. There can never be any statistical foundation for such an insurance. Most countries have acknowledged this by dropping the name "insurance," or at least by ignoring its implications. It has now become undisguised "assistance." It enables the trade unions to keep wages up to a rate at which only a part of those seeking work can be employed. Therefore, the assistance of the unemployed is what first creates unemployment as a permanent phenomenon. At present, many European states are devoting to the purpose sums that considerably exceed the capacity of their public finances.

The fact that there exists in almost every country permanent mass unemployment is considered by public opinion as conclusive proof that capitalism is incapable of solving the economic problem, and that therefore government interference, totalitarian planning and socialism are necessary. And this argument is regarded as irrefutable when people realize that the only big country which does not suffer from the evils of unemployment is communist Russia. The logic of this argument however, is very weak. Unemployment in the capitalist countries is due to the fact that the policy both of the governments and of the trade unions aims at maintaining a level of wages which is out of harmony with the existing productivity of labor. It is true that as far as we can see there is no large scale unemployment in Russia. But the standard of living of the Russian worker is much lower than the standard of living even of the unemployed dole receiver in the capitalist countries of the West. If the British or Continental workers were ready to accept wages which would indeed be lower than their present wages but which would still be several times higher than the wages of the Russian worker, unemployment would disappear in these countries too. Unemployment in the capitalist countries is not a proof of the insufficiency of the capitalist system, nor is the absence of unemployment in Russia a proof of the efficiency of the communist system. But the fact that there is unemployment as a mass phenomenon in almost every capitalist country is nevertheless the most formidable menace to the continuance of the capitalist system. Permanent mass unemployment destroys the moral foundations of the social order. The young people who, having finished their training for work, are forced to remain idle, are the ferment out of which the most radical political movements are formed. In their ranks the soldiers of the coming revolutions are recruited.

This indeed is the tragedy of our situation. The friends of trade unionism and of the policy of unemployment doles honestly believe that there is no way to ensure the maintenance of fair conditions of life for the masses other than the policy of the trade unions. They do not see that in the long run all efforts to raise wages above a level corresponding to the market reflection of the marginal productivity of the labor concerned must lead to unemployment, and that in the long run unemployment doles can have no other effect than the perpetuation of unemployment. They do not see that the remedies which they recommend for the relief of the victims—doles and public works—lead to consumption of capital, and that finally capital consumption necessitates a lowering of the wage level still further. Under present conditions it is clear that it would not be feasible to abolish the dole and the other less important provisions for the relief of the unemployed, public works and so on, at one single stroke. It is indeed one of the principal drawbacks of every kind of interventionism that it is so difficult to reverse the process—that its abolition gives rise to problems which it is almost impossible to solve in a completely satisfactory way. At the present day, the great problem of statesmanship is how to find a way out of this labyrinth of interventionist measures. For what has been done in recent years has been nothing else than a series of attempts to conceal the effects of an economic policy which has lowered the productivity of labor. What is now needed is first of all a return to a policy which ensures the higher productivity of labor. This includes clearly the abandonment of the whole policy of protectionism, import duties and quotas. It is necessary to restore to labor the possibility to move freely from industry to industry and from country to country.

It is not capitalism which is responsible for the evils of permanent mass unemployment, but the policy which paralyzes its working.

Notes

[1]Liek, *Der Arzt und seine Sendung,* 4th ed. (Munich, 1927), 54; Liek, *Die Schaden der sozialen Versicherung,* 2nd ed. (Munich, 1928), 17 et. seq., and a steadily growing mass of medical writings.